HUMANGEE 101

A MANUAL FOR UNDERSTANDING THE
HUMAN DEVICE

Published in 2020

GNF Ltd

See Disclaimer at rear

Publishing services provided by 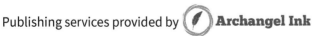 Archangel Ink

ISBN: 978-1-8382112-0-2

HUMANGEE 101

A MANUAL FOR LIVING

NOT FOR THE FAINT OF HEART

Contents

Author's Note

It's better than a lottery win, and it's there for anyone who really wants it …

That's the conclusion for this fifty-nine-year-old humangee, a student of life and of wisdom. Like many, he is an observer of human devices and of device interactions and collectives. He's observed that some enjoy their instrument and appreciate their environment while others don't. He writes this not with a judgmental tone but an inquisitive one.

This humangee, as a youngster like most others, went through the trials and tribulations of growing up, questioning everything from acne to church, from favoritism to bullying at school, from football to schoolwork and wondering about fitting in.

By the age of fifteen, on discovering that this device had some relative talent for athletics, he embarked on pursuing that with some vigor. With little interest in academics, he scraped into college but was more focused on what might be achieved through running. In relative international standard terms, he achieved modest results, enjoyed the adventure, and was frequently injured. After university, he got a post as a graduate assistant and studied for an MBA while continuing to pursue athletics. This is where an interest in sport psychology, facilitated by Dr. Bob McBrien, turned into an interest in wider self-help psychology in all its various forms.

Like many people moving into the career stage in their lives, this veered toward goal orientation, success-motivated and focused activity, and the drive to become "the person you are capable of becoming." Think Tony Robbins, Louis Tice, Brian Tracy, Stephen Covey, Wayne Dyer, and other personal development thought leaders at that time. He and his colleagues shared tapes and books, attended training, traveled to conventions, did firewalks, and more. There was not a blog, mp3, or podcast in sight, but the first mobile phones were in circulation.

By 1994, a colleague, Stanley Chambers, who was a positive psychology kindred spirit, had been to a set of classes in practical philosophy. Stanley indicated to this humangee and a friend, Martin McGeough, that they would enjoy it and find it useful. And so the next stage on the journey began. That was twenty-six years ago at roughly thirty-three years of age.

The choice and decision to study practical philosophy, or the love of wisdom, has had a huge impact on this man's life. It helped him piece all the other aspects from various thinkers together and has resulted in an enjoyable, contented, fulfilled, and blessed life. For this and more, he is very grateful.

His original tutor was a Mr. Shane Mulhall, a forty-something Dubliner who made the trip to Belfast every week. For him it was a six-hour round-trip journey at that time to deliver an introductory practical philosophy class, face to face, in a hotel conference room. He was also head of the school in Ireland. It was practical philosophy content facilitated with humor, lightness, pragmatism, and insight. From the first evening, this young-ish humangee was hooked.

Like any good teacher, Mr. Mulhall didn't just transmit relevant content but also the enthusiasm and the love of the subject. With regard to practical philosophy he was a great teacher—a humangee that exuded a set of characteristics and sensations that inspired the feeling "I want what you have." There was a contentment, and this teacher and his teachings were congruent with his actions.

The content in the classes was thought-provoking and not always easy to accept on the initial hearing. But each week the students did their exercises and came back for more.

While much of the previous physical and psychological training, discipline, and life experience had been useful in establishing a foundation, this content and process took it to another level.

It was simple and intuitive, sometimes challenging, but hugely practical. It focused on real observations (good and bad), challenges, and fun—the stuff of day-to-day life. It allowed the group collectively to shine a mirror on themselves, their interactions, and their lives, to test the concepts to establish whether they made sense. Invariably, they did make sense when considered in the light of real-world observation—in family life, in work, and in play.

Over time, it helped bind all the aspects together, where everything from religion, love, justice, anger, pleasure, fun, pain, relationships, stress, money, irritation, joy, death, work, compassion, misery, and life

interacted. When the rules and attributes were understood, they made perfect sense and enabled those who methodically explored them to appreciate a sensible whole. With this insight, the whole creation and interworking of the various aspects made seamless collective sense.

After nine years at the School of Practical Philosophy, this humangee tried putting into practice what he'd learned. It was a busy career time, his children were moving into secondary education, and more time was required for their needs. He stepped back from the school and spent more time with his wife and his children and on family activities during that next phase.

This unintentionally led him to coaching athletics for a further nine years, after which he returned to study practical philosophy in around 2014.

In 2016, Mr. Mulhall died. In recognition of his spirit of generosity and teaching, forty-three of the public lectures that he had delivered, including questions and answers, were made available by the school to all to share online. A commitment was made by this humangee to listen to these lectures and ensure that the wisdom was understood and incorporated into his daily living. He made some notes and determined to share the content and wisdom in a way that could make it more accessible to others. He considered creating a website, a blog, or a link to the audio content, but he eventually settled on writing this book.

Hopefully, it will make sense. For those interested in further study, resources are available online and around the globe to aid in investigating this vein of wisdom.

Regarding Humangee

A key tenet of practical philosophy, wisdom, and truth is the ability to see things clearly—to see things as they really *are* and not as how we *perceive* them through our current lenses. Hence, *humangee* came to life to provide a mechanism by which we might stand back from ourselves, become detached, and ask the more challenging questions. Hopefully, this dynamic can facilitate the search for better and more honest answers than we might otherwise achieve by direct naval gazing. Humangee is neither female nor male and is not distinguished by color, religion, country, or race. It's just the natural you.

Initial Acknowledgments

The principles in this manual are based largely on a distillation of philosophical observations over thousands of years. This includes numerous schools of thought, where the concepts are studied and tested in practical everyday living. It aligns with many of the great teachers, including Plato, Confucius, Lao Tzu, Christ, Muhammad, Buddha, Einstein, J Krishnamurti as well as current scientific, spiritual, and philosophical thought leaders and collectively with Advaita Vedanta philosophy.

Historically, many of these insights have been passed on by word of mouth, particularly when individuals went in search of the truth. In fact, the discipline of philosophy originated with students of wisdom going to these sages in search of truth and sharing their teachings over time.

Some of the quotations and teachings in this book come from conversations with Sri Śāntānanda Sarasvati and have been passed on verbally through conversations with members of the Study Society and the School of Practical Philosophy and their students over time. Many quotations are not directly attributable, so I offer here a collective thanks and acknowledgment to all those who have shared their input, insight, and wisdom.

Now in the twenty-first century, with YouTube, podcasts, and online interviews available, one does not need to travel to Nepal or visit an ashram in India to access this same wisdom. What is needed, however, is the context and clarification to piece the parts together and test and assimilate what is found to be true and useful. And, of course, the commitment to test it in practice and live the aspects that resonate with you for the good of all.

The search for answers

We can search high and low for our eyeglasses. Just like our questions about life, we may find that the answers and solutions are close at hand and are literally part of us.

Introduction

As humans, we are all allocated a piece of equipment, the humangee. This manual seeks to help you understand that device—less in the physical sense and more in the mental and software aspects, which ultimately control the instrument.

We start with the position that you are a *custodian* for the device and attempt to provide an objective view of the human use of mind in its environment. However, this relationship and description will evolve as you move through the manual, and the more subtle aspects of the software and being will become better understood over time.

This manual aims to enable you, the custodian, to better:

- understand your full device and mind.
- gain clarity on your position on Earth and in the human version of time.
- contextualize common misconceptions.
- gain clarity on natural laws.
- understand prevailing paradigms of life through exploring helpful ideas and terminology.
- unlock concepts that your device knows inherently.
- discover and use practical tools to assist your device in daily living.
- supplement other self-help books, podcasts, blogs, apps, and videos.

In doing so, this manual hopes to enable that life to be appreciated and enjoyed. If, on reading this book, you take appropriate action, you and your loved ones will find your lives changed for the better

forever. You might even consider keeping this manual in the smallest one-person sitting room in your dwelling (usually your bathroom)!

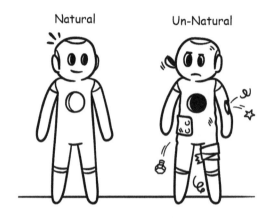

Natural   Un-Natural

Why is it called Humangee 101

A draft manual for living

There are many questions about humans, the mind, the body, and existence. Think back to studying English literature at school. Maybe you read a poem and then the class went line by line to dissect and analyze what the poet meant or intended.

Given the poet's background and place in time, what were the various things that may have influenced their observations? Who or what were they referring to, and what in their past life brought them to write this deep, insightful prose?

Following a discussion with a writer, they assessed that it was probably just a nice bright day where the poet experienced the circumstances differently than on another day. It was a fresh observation, written to express what they saw and felt. The thoughts and inspiration came to them, and within sixty minutes the draft was written.

Life, mind, and inner harmony are not unlike that (i.e., we can make something very complex out of something that is quite natural and simple). However, there is an innate knowledge that we need to be able to tap into, that we must learn to access. And there are paradigms and ground rules that need to be understood and set straight in order to achieve our natural harmonious state.

Hence the book is called *Humangee 101*, because in the US system of education, the 101 courses are generally the introduction level, which allow for the exploration of a specific topic or subject area. At this level, the course is designed to provide the core information to enable the student to establish whether they would like to investigate the subject further.

Humangee 101 was designed to serve the same purpose.

Ultimately, this manual aims to provide an overview that is understandable, relatable, and usable. It hopes to give the humangee enough information to decide if they would like to study and apply it more.

By virtue of buying this book, you have self-selected. You are self-motivated to find better answers to the bigger fundamental questions of life.

You are off to a good start. You will spend a lifetime with your humangee. How you

train, retrain, or manage it will set the tone and direction for the rest of your life.

Section 1 provides background knowledge and reframes some aspects of how we humans think about our device. It asks questions that you may or may not have considered and provides some references that may be helpful in ensuring a well-informed foundation for the material to follow. It also asks the questions from a perspective that stimulates a different view or appreciation. It may even convey a sometimes-helpful starting position, allowing the custodian to feel *I don't really know what I don't know*.

The chapters in section 2 detail the framework of how the humangee mind components operate. This provides explanation and recommendations for a happy, productive, contented life. These are based on sound principles, outlined throughout the manual.

A symbol in the footer of each page, and within the text, serves to act as a reminder to pause.

The icon comprises three buttons: *Pause* recommends moments of reflection throughout the day, *Go* reflects focused attention in activities, and *Stop* reflects complete rest and sleep when appropriate.

This pause may seem innocuous or irrelevant, but it is a mechanism for developing a habit of pausing regularly—learning to be awake, in the present, right now.

Consider it as the wedge of awakeness coming into your reading and mind activity. One of your tasks is to make a habit of pausing to come into the present moment (1–4 seconds is enough).

This manual is intentionally uncluttered. Therefore, many concepts lack examples and scenarios. This will no doubt leave gaps in understanding or make it seem devoid of clarifications.

However, unanswered questions are meant to be pursued by the user. As we know, it is only the answers that you are satisfied with that you will live by.

Good luck.

Section 1

Technical Comparisons and Overview

Chapter 1
Getting to Know HUMANGEE

It's your birthday. The first day of your life on planet Earth.

The device is wrapped up and primed for a whole new adventure.

It's like getting your own Puppy Humanoid Device.

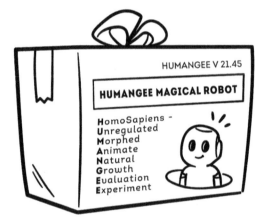

HUMANGEE V 21.45

HUMANGEE MAGICAL ROBOT

HomoSapiens - Unregulated Morphed Animate Natural Growth Evaluation Experiment

On the box it says:

Homo sapiens – **U**nregulated, **M**orphed, **A**nimate **N**atural **G**rowth **E**valuation **E**xperiment

Meeting Humangee

Humangee are provided free to parents and ultimately to the custodian. Parents generally take responsibility until a humangee is capable of fending for itself. At this stage in its life, it is helpful to really understand and appreciate the custodian's responsibilities. This is clarified throughout the manual and with some satire in the Software End Users License Agreement (EULA) in Appendix 3.

Word is that they are an advanced AI (Artificial Intelligence) robotic device capable of engaging in work, transportation, friendship, enjoyment, and more. There have been a few iterations to date. The specification of the hardware has now become relatively standard. Humangee has an extended-life battery that typically lasts up to eighteen hours before requiring recharging and a good emergency power backup system.

Humangee has a sophisticated bioengineering design with multiple interconnected and interdependent systems with remote failover systems. Hence, if one part is not operating properly, other components or systems may compensate. It has multiple input/output systems, a large and flexible random-access memory, and a superb storage system.

Not unlike a puppy at the start, humangee needs to be properly trained. If the unit is not managed correctly, it will develop inappropriate habits that are detrimental to itself, the custodian, and the wider community. If allowed to develop incorrectly, it has the capacity to become apathetic and lethargic. It will lose its spark, its sense of fun, and its ability to provide the joy and stimulation for which it was originally designed.

The description of and background to the name "humangee" is overviewed in chapter 3.

Beware Ego Virus

A frequent current problem is the development of Ego Virus, which causes the device to misinterpret reality and see ego and desire-driven outcomes as the aim. When humangee fails to fulfill these desires or encounters other challenges, their contentedness level drops below the healthy range.

This can be quite challenging for most, as they find it difficult to get the level back up once it has dropped. From an output perspective, if it has dropped, they will get up and go about their day-to-day activities but implement them in a less stimulated or joyous way than previously. Their interaction with others is somewhat muted, and they often experience a hint of resistance. For humangee, this can sometimes be tinged with disappointment and occasionally irritation.

Allowed to Evolve Naturally

The manufacturer-designer has historically not issued an owner's manual for the device, as it was keen to understand the full range of characteristics, personas, attributes, skills, and capacities that would evolve.

To date, natural changes have enabled devices to grow and evolve unconstrained in many aspects and develop unanticipated capabilities. The devices have uncovered a range of new modes of transport and ways of harvesting the fruits of nature on Earth.

Collectively, they have teamed together to solve very complex problems and to develop technological capabilities that are excellent and almost god-like.

Physical World versus Subtle World

In crude terms, there are two key realms in which humangee operate: the mind and the heart. These ultimately correspond to the physical and subtle worlds that we experience.

The physical world is the area where the thinking mind operates. It has evolved with human civilization and comprises that which we can appreciate and experience through the gates of our senses. It includes everything that we see, hear, and touch all around us. It includes the people and experiences we have on an everyday basis. We experience this physical world with our body and our mind. Parents and teachers encourage us to use our thinking mind. Throughout life and in school, through work and in university, we're taught or encouraged to think. We are taught that you need to think to survive or to get ahead. Over a lifetime, many humangee morph into thinking addicts, losing contact with or appreciation of what is going on in the heart.

Humangee wonder why there is misalignment in their thinking and actions; they wonder why discontentment arises that they cannot explain or comprehend.

By comparison, the subtle state is one of tranquility—presence without agitation. It is experienced in an absence of thought and desire. These characteristics of the heart are less well understood because we have been taught only to measure using our five senses and our externally focused thinking function. Hence, many people do not appreciate that this subtle aspect of our inner being exists and needs to be addressed and catered to. As the book progresses, we will show that the paradigm and picture painted by society is through a set of lenses that are not entirely accurate.

It is helpful for each humangee to consider the balance between the physical and subtle worlds, between the mind and heart. Should some form of equilibrium or alignment exist? And if it should, but is not accommodated, what are the consequences? Part of the purpose of this manual is to provide insight, to understand that this still, subtle state or aspect is accessible. It also presents tools on how to access, use, and enjoy it, and thus restore some balance.

Environment and Leadership Challenges

Individual humangee often make poor development and custodian choices, which have resulted in less-than-ideal device characteristics. Collectively, device communities have evolved with inconsistently implemented programming, not living by the original laws. For example, they only see one side of their being—the transient, changing, physical world part. They completely miss the permanent subtle world part.

This results in significant numbers of discontent humangee, doing increasingly self-sabotaging things. It is not necessarily helped that they are lacking well-informed role models, custodians, or wise leadership.

The net effect is a divergence from the design norms. The Ego Virus is spreading and is already yielding bad outcomes across the humangee database population. It,

along with other misconceptions, results in the humangee not appreciating its capability, its uses, or its purpose.

In essence, our poor humangee no longer knows who or what s/he is, or what s/he is capable of. This is a concern at one level, where it would be good to see if humangee can self-fix. If the virus continues unchecked, it has scope to destroy the Earth ecosystem and humangee life as we know it.

What is this EGO thing

I KNOW BEST. WHAT I WANT IS THE MOST IMPORTANT.

Discussing Our Humangee on a Third-Party Basis

Taking this approach as a human-like entity is helpful. As custodians, we have been given the opportunity to nurture, manage, have fun with, work with, enjoy, experiment with, share challenges with, spend time with, love, go through hard times with, and have total responsibility for humangee. The third-party view allows us to be more objective in how we look after another similar intelligent embodiment that has the same characteristics (namely ourselves).

We can even brush its teeth.

There is a mixing of reference to humangee, human, the being, and us, as we explore how best to manage the device and understand its environment (humangee is also the plural). These are all synonymous and interchangeable.

As the custodian, when these concepts have been read and understood, there is a clear direction and choice on whether to lead our humangee progressively to contentment or to a lesser alternative.

So, to start, we need to understand a bit about the basis on which the humangee has been designed and evolved.

In determining a true understanding of the more subtle aspects of the mind, we cannot use the same tools as for the physical sciences—measurement against sensory variables (sight, sound, feeling, taste, and smell). Neither can we use our known physical-world constants like gravity, the speed of light, measures of hardness, etc.

With regard to the subtle aspects of the mind and its functioning, we can use objective, awake, informed observational assessments of real examples from our daily lives, where the nuances and peripheral context is understood. In this way there is an appreciation of the scenarios, timing, history, impacts of various actions, and the associated outcomes.

Thus you can test principles for yourself and others over time to validate or refute the various concepts. Hence the positioning is that these principles are based on practical observations. The findings from this more subjective but voluminous critique process is consistent in the everyday lives of millions of humans over many years. It has been done by philosophers throughout history and is a core practice for the students of this area. Students on this path veer away from theory and become firmly grounded in practice, trials, tribulations, and minutiae—the reality of daily life. This is what makes it real, believable, acceptable, and thus actionable.

At a personal level, each individual needs to appreciate the nuances from their own perspective. Thus, it is paramount for each of us to do our own assessments and reach our own conclusions.

References to spirituality, religions, and concepts beyond what we can demonstrate by personal practical examples are minimized.

So, in simple terms, we know it works but not always why or how it works—maybe a bit like your mobile device.

Unboxing: This is the process when one gets a new bit of tech. Take it out of the box, remove the packaging, assemble it if needed, see it, hold it, find the instructions, and see how it works.

An Instrument for My Use

Humangee comprise more than just a body and a mind. The challenge and adventure is in understanding and using what they have.

Questions Determine Answers

It is vital to appreciate that the questions that we ask ourselves determine the type of answers that we get (e.g., Why are you so bad at this? What is wrong with you today?)

If we repeatedly ask the same questions, we get the same type of answers. Most humangee become habitual in the nature and type of questions they ask.

If we ask better or different questions, we get better or different answers (e.g., What are you most enthused about today? What are you most thankful for at the moment? I'm curious, what insight prompted you to reach that conclusion?)

To help us see a bit more clearly, the questions in the following sections are simply to provoke some thought into how you look at your device and help uncover some aspects of how it might operate.

Another way of looking at the questions (and our answers to them) is as a mechanism to muddy the water or scratch the mental record in what we ask of ourselves, as we will then see things in a different and broader way than before. We then have some scope to be even more open-minded or to see from other perspectives.

Understanding the Fundamentals

Consider a humangee a bit like a fantastic spaceship with lots of controls, buttons, and capabilities. Once you've unpacked it, what would you do with it?

You might look for an on/off button. Look at the controls to see how you can make it start. Is there a brake or a handbrake, should you want to stop it in a hurry? You may even look for a manual or instructions or ask your parents how it operates. However, they might only be able to understand it a bit more than you, if at all.

You would want to know how it works, what it can do, and what it is designed for. How fast can it go? Are the models that other people have different? What aspects are the same as others' instruments? How can it be useful to me, my friends, my family?

Where should we keep it? Does it need fuel? Once I have it going, what if some part breaks? What do I do, who do I go to? Who is my mechanic or support person?

How does this thing work?

Computing Device Aspects

What about the software operating system— how is it managed and kept up to date? What apps does it run, or can it run? If it has an inappropriate program or virus, can I remove it? Is there an antivirus or anti-malware application?

What about security. Can the instrument be phished or hacked? Can other people mess with my applications? Can others see, corrupt, or interfere with my data or programs?

Whether you appreciate it or not, you are the custodian of a phenomenally dexterous, functional, robotic device. Even more relevant, it is a sophisticated piece of computing, storage, and communicating equipment! If managed properly, it will serve you well, but if not, it may not operate the way you would like.

Device Network and Applications

How does my instrument receive inputs and data? How does it output, store, and communicate with others? Do these instruments only communicate on a very local basis (e.g., with Bluetooth), with Wi-Fi in my house/office or immediate vicinity, or with 4G/5G—on all of the time to a wider network?

Is there a wider communication capability among humangee devices or instruments? Are there any central servers in operation or applications that all humangee instruments can avail themselves of?

Do we have a World Wide Web or a mental Facebook, Amazon, or Netflix? Is there a place or process where we get the mental, emotional, and spiritual stuff we need? Is management of the system centralized or decentralized?

How do I fuel or recharge my device? Should I turn it off at night? How do I know if the charge is low? Does it have different stores of charge? Which WhatsApp groups do I share my data, interests, and thoughts with?

The human instrument has physical aspects that I can see, feel, hear, sense, and touch. But more importantly, it has significant other aspects that are subtle or hidden under the various covers or compartments. These are the ones where there is less clear direction on how they operate and should or could be managed.

Invest the time & effort to learn how to manage your device

The great news is you CAN learn how to manage it.

You'll be glad to hear that, like a car or a mobile phone, when you know how to use it, you can have hours, years, and decades of fun and adventure.

However, if you don't learn to drive and manage it, if you don't live by the natural laws—like an incompetent, albeit well-meaning, vehicle driver—you will end up either crashing, being crashed into, or drifting into a ditch.

If this happens, will you be able to get up and out on the open road again to tell the tale? Some will learn a bit of how to manage and control the device. Most choose to drive with the radio on, phone in hand, the windshield obscured with mist and dust, focusing on the peripherals, with low attention or focus on the proper path or road. As a result of poor guidance, most humangee are subject to a constant state of trial and error, hoping for the best.

To use the old cliché: Hope is not a good strategy.

A parallel comparison with a software-based device that we all know and love is helpful, as it allows us to use a recognized concept when explaining the benefits of learning to use the device. We now have a generation of "phone dependents," those who can't live without their handset.

Your humangee makes the Apple-Galaxy Home Robot, due to launch in 2046, seem like a child's toy.

Your device is singularly one of the best designed pieces of equipment and operating environments ever. And what's more, we all get one for free. And the game is to learn how to use it for survival, enjoyment, and the common good.

Chapter 2
Specifications and Overview

For Humangee Software End Users License Agreement, see Appendix 3 (***requires consent agreement***).

Software and Hardware[1]

- Hardware version 21.4 CMV
- Software version 2.11.5
- Input senses: standard
- (visual, auditory, touch, taste,
- olfactory, sixth)
- Output devices (as above): as standard
- Wireless receivers: standard
- Wireless emitters: standard
- Weight and dimensions: vary by allocation
- Finishes, distinctive features: vary by allocation
- Unique variations: vary by allocation
- Core HOS (human operating system): standard
- Human inner AI-interface core: standard
- All other components: standard, based on natural variants
- Universal cloud access: yes
- Communication and energy modules: standard
- Fueling, disposal, reproductive, respiratory, pulmonary, filtration, and other systems: standard

This device is a fabulous self-teaching, self-regulating, self-learning piece of multifunctional equipment.

Hey, so you have been given a life (a humangee) with one of the fabulous 21CMV (Twenty-First Century Model Variant) units. You were lucky enough to be born in the second half of the twentieth century or early 2000s.

What you have is a very standard piece of kit: the basic framework and structure is largely unchanged from earlier recent versions. The core operating system and component architecture are still the same. The same tried-and-tested biological systems are in these great new models. These are explained in numerous other books on the body and have a strong following in the medical fraternity. However, there are important changes to the operating environment that have exposed some weaknesses in application performance areas.

The current variant is limited to the six sense organs provided, and is thus incapable of some of the capabilities of other species. Humangee does not have the nano lens optical devices or the ultrasonic or multifrequency audio devices, neither do they have the optional low-level energy receptor module as yet.

---

1 Generally dependent on allocation to each custodian.

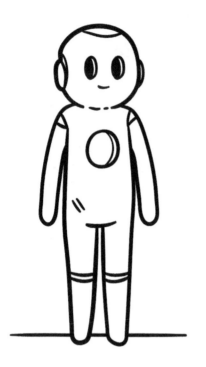

stimulation of "the desire to have things beyond our core needs."

These TV devices originally occupied one room in the house, so they still allowed some form of inter-humangee conversation and sharing of content. However, this has further evolved and transformed to our current media consumption over the inter-net years. It is now dominated by singular devices, primarily mobile phones, that each humangee is often attached to. We will look at this area in more detail later. The main point at this stage is that there has been a shift to humangee independence (doing things for and by oneself) and away from interdependence (doing things with and for others). This has had significant effects on relationship development and transfer of critical device management skills for the humangee.

The terms *device* and *instrument* are used interchangeably.

One key change that has evolved over the last period is the change in user awareness training and support. Historically, previous user generations received training and support in their home and community environment, primarily by "voice–listening interaction." Also known as *word of mouth*, this often occurred between generations and other influencers like teachers.

A Huge Increase in Mental "Noise"

This has changed in recent years with the advent of television and other media, which introduced "noise" in the wider sense of the word, including advertisements. These essentially developed to show people what they don't have and sell them things that they may or may not need. This was prob-ably the key starting point for the dramatic

Minimal or No Training

The 21CM variants tend to get minimal training or user support and often operate without a user manual.

A bit like the new phone devices, some of the instructions can be found online. But in the case of the 21CMV human device, quality direction and advice can be chal-lenging to find and is buried piecemeal in other content. Good guidance is not necessarily clearly specified and validated in a centralized place. And often by the time it is found, it is late—bad habits have formed and are well embedded. Resetting the device to develop the disciplines is a complicated task by that point.

The downside for most custodians is that many do not know what their instrument is for, why they have it, and what they should do with it. Thus, fewer people are able to make full use of their instrument, and they struggle to live the happy and productive lives they could and should.

Blind lead the blind

Partial truths are built upon assumptions, resulting in misinformation, which is then layered on more misinformation from another area or aspect. In the same way we have a challenge distilling the truth from the spectrum of daily news we receive—ranging from truth to fake news and blatant lies—we also need to be cognizant of distilling the truth in internal guidance ranging from true wisdom to uninformed tips. In the end, we're confused and don't know where to turn or who to believe.

What is a humangee? What is the baseline? Why is this important?

In the conventional approach, the fundamentals of what the instrument is for—and how the subtle aspects of mind, heart, and soul work—are not properly explained. Consequently, there is limited understanding of our fundamental aspects, and thus no consistent baseline. Hence the resulting collective understanding is chaotic and generally not just of low utility and value but positively harmful for proper informed insight and intelligent use. And further, users are less informed on the humangee's intended use and how to achieve steady progression.

There are those who have had some exposure to the principles and disciplines. There are some who know what to do but don't do it consistently. And then others generally fit into the category of, "I know what to do, so why can't I do it?"

The reality is relatively simple:

a. We don't fully appreciate how humangee operates and the implications of

Current options for guidance are ad-hoc and often of poor quality.

We have body, mind, and some other aspects that are not yet well understood. So … what do we do to bridge the knowledge gap?

We can go to others for advice about operating our instrument, but they may be equally in the dark. This is not a scientifically objective or helpful approach.

Here, the blind lead the blind. Well-meaning instrument custodians share their experiences—think an online user forum or Twitter cluster made up of uninformed well-meaning enthusiasts.

Attempts are made to come up with best-effort instructions and support collateral that the manufacturer and their service support team could or should have provided in the first place.

the "law of unintended consequences" in this realm.

b. We don't take the necessary reset steps. These are, in truth, practical and simple, though not necessarily easy to habitualize in our preconditioned world.

The good news is that there is a body of philosophical and observational work and insight built up over generations designed to address these very issues. But it is so far removed from where we are now that many of the aspects seem alien to our current paradigms and conditioning.

Conventional Medical, Scientific, and External Body-Mind Approach

In line with mankind's scientific approach to our universe, our planet, and the humans living on it, there has been a significant set of advancements in the medical, psychological, and psychiatric disciplines. However, there are still gaps in understanding of humangee learning and development that result in a significant mental health deficit across the planet.

There are practitioners who understand some aspects of mental illness to varying degrees. There are humangee trained in the systems and numerous ailments that are encountered within this sphere.

There are plenty of sources of information and trained medical practitioners and specialists for literally every centimeter of our physical body.

As mentioned elsewhere, the focus of our medical system is not on prevention or preparation. It is primarily in response to events, disease, and trauma. And the approach to the software and mental aspects is reactive rather than proactive.

So, when software and mental problems arise, the counselors, therapists, psychiatrists, and psychologists are tasked with fixing the problem. Firstly, it's very late in the day and, secondly, patients abdicate responsibility for health in this realm. The net effect is that the role of these therapists is challenging and requires pushing against some deeply rooted misunderstandings and misalignments.

Additionally, they work with a range of assumptions and an assortment of crude tools. There are drug companies, food conglomerates, physical trainers, coaches, gym clubs, universities, blogs, and more— all doing their best, each giving their spin on aspects of the human body-mind, its ailments, and its interaction with the creation. One of the many challenges is the profusion of mixed messages. And even if the remedies were consistent, most mature humangee would have difficulty implementing them.

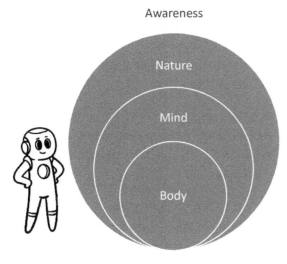

Awareness

Nature

Mind

Body

A basic model to consider

The objective of this manual is to establish a workable user guide based on fundamentals with clear, validated instructions on how to appreciate and use the more complex aspects of the device.

This manual aims to help users understand their software, or the non-visible and more subtle aspects of the device, and get pointers on where to go for support or repairs.

You may find some parts challenging. And that is good, because it is pushing you to review your beliefs to establish what is actually true.

Frequently, we find that older custodians (users over fourteen) have become so accustomed to incorrect use of their device that they find it difficult to change, reboot, or refine their settings. It can be done, but it does take work. It is well worth it.

The parallel of trying to teach grannies and grandads how to operate mobile phones spring to mind. ☺

Fundamentals and Misconceptions

If you think that you and your humangee are just a body and a brain, you are selling yourself WAY short.

It's a bit like saying your smartphone is just a collection of metal, plastic, computer chips, electronic components, a bit of see-through glass, and software to make it work. This may be physically true, but it still undervalues the utility, components, versatility, and capability of the device, as well as the synergy enabled with other devices.

In the coming chapters, we explore the questions: What is a humangee? What is its purpose? How may the custodian manage it?

A useful starting point is realizing that although your body is the bit that you see and live in, it is essentially a subset of, and subservient to, your mind, nature, and more.

So, in simple crude terms, we could say that your physical body-device is like your mobile phone. It has an operating system and applications, which include your mind and your nature.

With your phone, you access the global central resource via your data connection, either 3G/4G/5G, Wi-Fi, or Bluetooth, and you are connected via internet and cellular networks to other devices. With humangee, a core network of equally huge capacity and value can be accessed also. But many are unaware how to properly access or use it.

A Basic History

If we start with several thousand years of a growing population on Earth, from the evolution of *Homo sapiens* up to today, humangee have collectively built systems of knowledge gained by insight as they saw it at the time.

How humans have perceived their instrument and their world and how they have communicated has changed over time. Humans of the past had a more intimate connection with the Earth and its operation and subtleties. They also had a less "noisy" observation and interaction with the body-mind instrument and its environment (i.e., they had fewer distractions and complications than we do today).

It's not unreasonable to say that they were more in tune with their surroundings and nature than we are today.

Over the last two hundred years there has been an explosion of content or sharable knowledge made widely available. What started as a relatively small number of books and publications and limited radio, TV, or video content has expanded to allow us access to a much deeper and broader pool of information. We now can access nearly all of the sciences, with discoveries across physics, chemistry, biology, sociology, anthropology, philosophy, and the human body over the years. These have led to developments and life-on-Earth changes that were inconceivable in the 1800s.

Some would say we know more but understand less, or know the price of everything but not the value.

Despite the ways we've evolved in terms of physical world content or knowledge, there is a question of whether we are awake or in touch with our inner being and the internal aspects that determine us.

Our physical and cerebral aspects may have evolved in the last two centuries, but relative to the changes man has made on Earth, it is a miniscule variation.

We are a sophisticated designer primate, shaved and clothed, with a mind that still runs the same core operating system as it did thousands of years ago. In itself, that is not a bad thing. But it would be useful to appreciate how it works.

If I Can't See It, It Doesn't Exist

Two hundred years ago, we didn't know of electricity. The concept of "electric power" was incomprehensible, let alone the idea that every home could harness the magical utility. The concept that some invisible force could travel unseen and make lights work at will was laughable. Furthermore, this force could be used to support all types of machines that could generate heat exactly when we need it, without having to make a fire. It could be used for cooking. You could even harness it with a device for drying your wet hair.

The same theory-to-reality shift has happened in numerous other fields from radio technology to chemical analysis, from medical and technical imaging to the ability to fly from one place to another. The list is huge and ever-expanding.

Regarding the operation of physical beings, including animals, we knew little about how things operated at a more subtle physical level. We are now becoming more familiar with quantum physics and the operation of energies within and between the species.

Humangee see the physical world and have been taught to understand aspects of it, albeit at a superficial level. However, what is not seen, not properly acknowledged, not appreciated as they could be are the invisible, inaudible, and subtle aspects of ecosystems, of the plants, species, and humans.

The Observer

A key aspect to consider here is that you realize that you can observe your body, so you are not just your body; you are more than your device. And something can observe your mind seeing your body; you are not just your body-mind. You are more, much more.

In the next few chapters we will begin to peel back the layers to help you discover what you really are.

A bit like finding a light that is hidden and dimmed under layers of dust, grime, and inadvertent coverings.

Who Observes the Humangee

ARE THEY ABLE TO DRIVE IT?

DO THEY KNOW THE RULES?

Another Turning Point in Time

We are all aware of the effect of the internet and of electronic devices—how they have changed the way we learn and communicate with other humans. Unfortunately, our memory muscles have atrophied as a result of lower requirement for recall—now that we rely on a search engine, an online tool, or a map to find a thing or place. Our capacity and daily need for things like mental arithmetic and pictorial and other memory has diminished. The ability and fluency for handwriting among the younger generation continues to decrease. Our appreciation for and prioritizing of "mental downtime and rest" has diminished significantly.

Future

So, life has changed in innumerable ways, some for better and some for worse. While we've seen significant advances in some mental, subtle, and cerebral areas, there has been a very definite step backward in others.

In thirty years' time, the device will be even better understood. Maybe the software and operating environment will be better appreciated. Particularly the benefit of understanding self-management its positive and negative outcomes—based on adoption or rejection of relatively simple laws and rules.

This manual aims to help humangee learn to live in the present, to wake up (more in chapter 9) one at a time, and to see reality and the many positive options that are available in a lifetime, that they may choose to see the play of life (more in chapter 4) for what it really is.

In *The Life and Times of the Thunderbolt Kid*, Bill Bryson explains that, according to the Gallup Organization, 1957 was the happiest year ever recorded in the United States of America. The giddy peak of American bliss saw entry into a world where things were done because they offered a better return, not a better world. He writes, "People were wealthier than ever before, but life somehow didn't seem as much fun. The economy had become an unstoppable machine…. what had once been utterly delightful was now becoming very slightly, rather strangely unfulfilling. People were beginning to discover that joyous consumerism is a game of diminishing returns."

By the end of the 1950s most middle-class people had achieved and acquired pretty much everything they'd dreamed of, so they set out to buy more and bigger versions of things that they didn't truly need: "second cars, lawn tractors, double-width fridges, hi-fis with bigger speakers and

more knobs to twiddle, extra phones and televisions, room intercoms, gas grills, kitchen gadgets, snowblowers, you name it. Having more things of course also meant having more complexity in one's life, more running costs, more things to look after, more things to clean, more things to break down. Women increasingly went out to work to help keep the whole enterprise afloat. Soon millions of people were caught in a spiral in which they worked harder and harder to buy labor-saving devices that they wouldn't have needed if they hadn't been working so hard in the first place."[2]

A Rudderless Being

While we have a physical instrument and an externally changing environment, the more significant part of our existence is controlled by our software and experienced, managed, lived internally "in our head."

Most of our identity and focus is on the physical body, and "who we are." However, in relative terms, it is purely a piece of hardware that is essentially a transport vehicle for our mind, heart, nature, and essence, with sensory input/output capabilities.

The software is what drives and determines the life.

---

2 Bill Bryson, *The Life and Times of the Thunderbolt Kid: A Memoir* (New York: Broadway Books, 2006)

Aimless
wandering humangee

Some questions to consider:

1. What is your true nature?
2. Is it helpful to know what your device is for?
3. Is it helpful to know what it needs and what it doesn't?
4. How do you control, use, and manage it on an ongoing basis?
5. How should you best manage the instrument in different circumstances?
6. What do instruments/devices have in common?
7. Do you appreciate that humangee have an essence that is integral to our device?

In the absence of knowing what we are and what we are here for, and without knowing our true nature, we are a blind humangee.

Is There a Set of Guidelines?

Are there guidelines that apply to the instrument and humangee species on Earth? This is a hugely important question and one that is worthy of some of our time and energy. If there are guidelines, it could have huge implications on the quality of our life—and use of this instrument.

Based on practical experience garnered over millions of years of human civilization, we have some pointers.

We can start with a set of principles or laws that apply universally to humankind. Students of the subtle aspect of the instrument conclude that these laws and their consequential aspects apply. However, it is vital that the custodian of each humangee tests their own understanding of these principles.

In section 2 of this manual, you'll be guided through many of these principles and laws. It is recommended that you literally challenge everything about the ideas you currently hold on the areas covered in section two. If you are thorough in this activity, the conclusions you reach will be in total alignment with your being.

Just like learning to drive a car, one must become comfortable with using the controls and understanding the rules of the road. One needs to appreciate the interaction with other vehicles on the road and their associated drivers. So, a key starting point is to challenge all your preconceived opinions and beliefs from a place of conscious awareness. Some of these are considered in this manual. Take this opportunity to test key beliefs in light of your lived experience, to ascertain what is true and what may be false.

You can read a book or use an online app to learn about car driving theory, but it's not until you get into a car and drive on the road that it becomes real. After that, you can drive a car properly and safely on the open road with other drivers and adhere to the rules of the road.

The same applies to driving and managing your humangee properly.

In reference to the availability of guidelines, moral codes, religious and spiritual beliefs, and traditions are handed on from one generation to the next (see chapter 5 for more). These traditions provide huge value in one regard, in that they pass on many useful practices to the masses and should be an excellent foundation for living and applying the laws. But there are some practices passed down without review that don't hold up against true fundamental laws. Secondly, many of the people who subscribe to these religions are not necessarily true practitioners in the accurate sense of the word.

To conclude, there are a range of guidelines put forward by various groups, each with pros and cons. The medium for passing on the sentiment has changed. There is a gap and a need to make it simpler, current, honest, and more effective.

Chapter 3

Humangee: A Product of Nature

This chapter sets out that the human (and thus humangee) is a product of nature. It is an output of the natural systems that exist on Earth and subject to the same parameters that determine natural existence over millennia.

What Is the Natural System?

The Earth and nature are demonstrated clearly by our biosphere or ecosphere. These comprise the collective biological and physical components of the planet that aggregate to make all of our ecosystems. This includes plants, animals, insects, microscopic life, land, sea, air, climate and weather systems, and natural resources. It is the zone of life on the planet, which operates essentially as a closed system, apart from solar and cosmic radiation and heat from the earth's core.

Like its many inhabitants, it is largely self-regulating, and all the systems work autonomously. There is a symbiotic relationship between the various ecosystems that helps maintain balance. The land supports plants, trees, vegetation, and agriculture, which are in turn supported by insects, pollination, and other processes and enable consumption and use by various animals including humangee. Everything operates in natural cycles, and nothing is wasted. Natural products have a life cycle, after which they return to whence they came. It is an efficient and complete system that follows natural laws. Humangee are an integral part of those ecosystems.

Evolution and Humangee

The following brief evolution summaries map out the starting observations and origins of life on Earth and progress onto plants, living creatures, and ultimately to *Homo sapiens* and human beings or humangee.

These are for background information and context and can be skipped as appropriate.

Transformation of the Planet

Rather than go right back to the very start, we will start around 1.6 billion years ago. It is now clear that Earth was once an inhospitable planet, just like many others in our solar system. It did not support life as we now know it. The specific change event is not conclusive, as with any distant history. However, one of a few process candidates was responsible for initiating the change. A genetic analysis of the genome of the cyanobacteria pro-

---

vided the essential clues to the transition from a hostile-to-life globe into the lush, naturally evolved planet that we have the privilege of inhabiting today.

These studies clarified the origin of a chain of events whereby a single cell started the metamorphosis via the initiation of photosynthesis in plants. A tiny alga apparently combined with a bacterium and enabled the harnessing of energy from the sun. In essence, it became the first basis for a plant and the Earth's first solar power plant—excuse the pun.

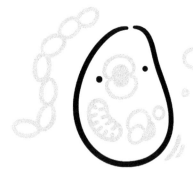

*A nascent organelle—source
of an original plant*

These findings and conclusions were reached by an international consortium of scientists studying the genetics of a collection of unique microscopic blue-green algae, known as living fossils. There is much more detail on the nature of the bacterium, as well as analysis in the scientific journals, including in *Scientific American*. The work suggests that all plants are essentially hybrids pieced together from the bits evolved from this union.

This development, along with others, facilitated the development of the ozone layer, which exists in the Earth's stratosphere approximately 15–35 km above the surface. It is created by ultraviolet light striking ordinary oxygen molecules containing two oxygen atoms (O_2), splitting them into individual oxygen atoms (atomic oxygen). What follows then is a continuing process called the ozone–oxygen cycle.

The ozone layer or shield is a region of Earth's stratosphere that absorbs most of the sun's ultraviolet radiation.

It is another fortuitous evolution that protects life on Earth from many of the harmful effects of the sun's rays. Over time, these changes and others have enabled a supergroup of extremely successful organisms (i.e., the plants) to develop.

Evolution of Life, Humans, and Humangee

The following high-level overview provides a few of the known evolutionary milestones. It clearly sets out how humans have evolved from their early ancestral roots—a simple bacteria. It is provided in the context of understanding how things really are, based on verifiable findings, rather than what we may have been led to believe.

3.8 Billion Years Ago (BYA) is our current estimate for the beginning of life on Earth when a common ancestor gave rise to two main groups of life: bacteria and archaea. The following are rough guides to years and the associated state of animal life evolution.

2.15–1.6 BYA: First fossil evidence of cyanobacteria and photosynthesis. This indicates the ability to take in sunlight and carbon dioxide and obtain energy, releasing oxygen as a by-product. Eukaryotic cells, cells with internal "organs," emerge.

1.5–1.0 BYA: The eukaryotes divide into three groups: the ancestors of modern plants, fungi, and animals.

500–450 Million Years Ago (MYA): Fossil evidence shows that animals were exploring the land at this time. The great Ordovician biodiversification event leads to a great increase in diversity. Within each of the major groups of animals and plants, many new varieties appear. Plants begin colonizing the land. Fish split into two major groups: the bony fish and cartilaginous fish.

400–350 MYA: The first four-legged animals, or tetrapods, evolve. They go on to conquer the land and give rise to all amphibians, reptiles, birds, and mammals. The oldest fossilized tree dates from this period.

300–200 MYA: The pelycosaurs, the first major group of synapsid animals, dominate the land. Therapsids evolve alongside them and eventually replace them and evolve into the first mammals. The Permian period ends with the greatest mass extinction in Earth's history. The ecosystem recovers and undergoes a change. The sauropsids now take over, in the form of dinosaurs. Ancestors of

mammals survive as small nocturnal creatures.

150–100 MYA: Archaeopteryx, the famous first bird, lives in Europe. Around this time, placental mammals split from their cousins the marsupials. The first flowering plants emerge, following a period of rapid evolution.

75–64 MYA: The ancestors of modern primates split from the ancestors of modern rodents and lagomorphs. Grasses evolve. The Cretaceous–Tertiary extinction wipes out a swath of species, including the dinosaurs. The extinction clears the way for the mammals, which go on to dominate the planet.

64–50 MYA: The primates split into two groups known as the haplorhines and the strepsirrhines. The strepsirrhines become lemurs, while the haplorhines develop into monkeys and apes—and humans.

50–40 MYA: The well-known fossilized primate known as "Ida" lives in northern Europe.

40 MYA: A subgroup of monkeys become the first simians (higher primates) to diverge from the rest of the group.

25–7 MYA: Apes, gibbons, and gorillas split off at various times.

6 MYA: Humans separate from the chimpanzees and bonobos, their closest relations, and by 1 MYA hominins begin walking on two legs.

The next stage of history began.

Evolution of Humangee

Nature's Designs

Nature demonstrates the ultimate in purity. It is efficient and refined, and in some aspects, it appears ruthless and cruel. It is a life-seeking force that is constrained by its own natural laws. It has enabled a catalyst event to evolve into a set of balanced ecosystems. It is stunning, awesome, simple in some ways and hugely complex in others. Its beauty and refinement are mirrored in humangee. It is responsible for evolving our planet and its associated environment and systems, including its animals.

This is vital to understand and appreciate.

Humangee are naturally evolved creatures, and we need to understand our origins, evolution, and makeup. This goes beyond DNA, physiology, psychology. It goes to the very essence of our being.

Humangee is an evolved animal with a set of guiding principles that determine its operation.

Aligning with Earth and Nature or Not

That which applies to nature applies to humangee. So, in our physical, externally focused Earth lives, we focus on the challenges of day-to-day living and interaction with other humangee. However, if we want to make the best use of our awake time on this planet, it is helpful to understand our underlying mechanisms and constraints. Like the Earth, plants, ecosystems, and other animals, our functioning is constrained by natural processes and laws. We may have benefited from a much higher level of evolved intelligence, but we still need to understand the effects of going against the grain with our thoughts or of fighting against our inner nature.

If we do not understand our underpinning natural wiring, how we are designed to operate, then we will keep meeting unnecessary and unhelpful situations and dissatisfaction.

So, next time you come across a challenging event or problem, you have the choice to look at it in multiple ways. One choice is a form of acceptance. If we refer to the cliché "It is what it is," we can see the reality of the current situation for what it is. We are then in a position to choose from available options on how best to respond or progress.

A classic expression of this is that, to the extent that we cannot accept things, we will experience internal friction. The beauty of this understanding is that the choice to accept reality or not is a completely conscious, self-determined choice.

It is helpful to appreciate what is within our control and what is not. Like a windsurfer, we cannot change the wind, but we can adjust our sail.

Aligned or Misaligned to Our Natural Composition

If we take it to its extreme, there are a set of guidelines:

- On the one end, one is totally aligned with the natural way, fully awake, wise, and thus blissfully content.
- At the other end, there is a set of beliefs and paradigms—what may be called misconceptions—where one is purely focused on the human play, on the external world, and is driven by selfish, personal, ego-based thinking.

These extremes are tabulated in Appendix 4 to convey the difference in approach and the direction that each paradigm takes the humangee individually and in groups, at a small, medium, and large level (i.e., progressing in size from family, community, organization or company, to country or global population).

The macrocosm reflects the microcosm or the larger ecosystem reflects the smaller component parts. That is, the outer expression reflects the inner.

So, for humangee, the outer manifestation—whether appearance, enthusiasm, aura, etc.—reflects the state of what is going on inside. In the same way that some may say that the eyes are the window to the soul, it could be said that the humangee that we see and encounter is a reflection of what's going on within.

As without, so within.

The same applies across the levels as we move to larger groups. The organization becomes a reflection of the leadership or the culture. This is why culture, mission and values, and leadership within companies and organizations is so important. It has a fundamental impact on the "nature of the organization." The same goes for countries and their leaders and government.

Humangee Hierarchy of Needs

Humangee are born into the Earth world. There are some basic necessities that need to be met in order for life to proceed successfully.

The basic body requirements are addressed first. Then body and mind must be tended to. There are aspects to manage in the relationship area. After these have been addressed, higher considerations like happiness, truth, and freedom can be sought.

As humangee meet the needs of each level, there is a daily environmental peer-pressure that pushes or pulls humangee to have wants rather than simply the needs it had before that.

Humangee has the opportunity to be awake to these thoughts and must realize how to tread a balanced path between these needs and wants.

Some wants are fine. What is important is the intent and attachment. Constant vigilance is required to determine one's intent and attachment to these needs and wants.

1. Body	2. Body & Mind	3. Tribe	4. Fulfillment
Survival needs, food, water, sleep, basic clothing, somewhere to live, safety	Security of resources, work, money or other capacity to support self, family and health	Companions, fitting in, and being accepted, family and close relationships	Awareness; ability to be present, still, attentive and mindful, grateful, happy, free

Natural needs and prioritized preferences—based loosely on Maslow's hierarchy of needs

This is particularly important for the "householder" (i.e., someone who has dependents). Humangee could have a spouse who sees the path differently from them. Maybe they desire status, property, and wealth accumulation beyond appropriate need. This will be an opportunity to learn and practice the disciplines outlined in the later chapters and appendices.

Earning a Living

As an evolved animal, we're designed to find food and shelter, to eat, rest, live in groups, and more. Given how our humangee society has evolved, we generally need to find money to live within our modern community. This has progressed for many adults of the species to the extent where we need to spend much of our time getting sufficient money to live to ensure our survival. Often two or more members of the family may need to forage for enough money to provide for the household. This results in a very clear orientation to meet this need and to protect what has been collected. The principles that we cover later will show other ways to look at this and how to be much more effective in this area.

Natural Planet, Natural Systems, Natural Laws

One of the key takeaways from this chapter is that we live in a world that has evolved and exists under a natural system of rules and principles. This nature applies and determines our existence. If we appreciate it and align ourselves with it, then we are in harmony with nature. If we are asleep or think it's not relevant to us, then there is friction and dissonance, and things don't work as harmoniously.

The term dissonance is apparently derived from "dis-one-ance," meaning "not one." Contrary to unity, oneness, and alignment, which facilitate harmony, dissonance encapsulates the concept of duality, lack of alignment or harmony.

Humangee Conundrum or Challenge

A challenge or conundrum of the natural design is that the humangee identifies with its local body-mind, which appears to push it toward external things. Things that it can see and experience and show to its peers. It focuses primarily on these for security, pleasure, and reward in the expectation of happiness and contentment. This is where the challenges start.

Like other challenges, when you can see and understand the test, then you have some scope to be able to do something about it.

Selfishness

Humangee has evolved with self-preservation as a core instinct, and the current net effect of this is a tendency toward selfishness. This needs to be understood and managed. Without understanding or utilizing its true nature and capacity, it can have a tendency to self-sabotage and undermine its own capabilities.

Humangee are innately insecure, especially in the early stages of life. The route taken by humangee in the absence of an awake custodian becomes misaligned with its true nature, resulting in dissatisfaction and undermining its own capabilities.

So the job of this manual now is to help you appreciate the custodian role and be present and awake more of the time.

Natural Processes

The Earth and its inhabitants all form part of a set of natural processes. These processes or interactions generally involve moving energy or nutrients from one place to another. Examples of natural processes include weathering and decomposition, sediment transport and soil formation, and the many forms of plant and animal interactions, climate, and natural disturbances like storms, floods, and fires, reproduction, and regeneration cycles. They all create mechanisms to move nutrients, energy, or both.

The water cycle depending on where one starts. Water in the form of rain, falls on land to form rivers, lakes, ponds, aquifers, and more. Ultimately, it works its way through various uses back through land, to be consumed by plant or animal species back toward the sea and oceans. Then it moves in a cycle with climate and geography back as rain or some form of precipitation.

The duration and scale of the processes vary hugely, from the level of an individual plant, to whole communities at once, such as through the provision of groundwater. Some natural processes occur in days, such as fires and floods, where others can take hundreds or thousands of years—such as the decomposition of a plastic bag.

Natural processes are a huge and complex interconnected ecosystem, with known and unknown interdependencies. Changes in one process can influence another or others. A change in water availability or pollution can create both known and unknown consequences, which also have secondary effects, often affecting whole communities of plant and animal species.

Loss of any natural capability in nature or in humangee represents some loss in function. These apparently minor losses of capability are often cumulative (i.e., they build on each other to achieve more substantial impacts).

Chapter 4
Eternal Laws

Establishing a Useful Starting Point

Have you ever tried to drive to a destination that you had never visited before and didn't know anything about? Can you remember how many times you lost your way or missed a turn?

You possibly had to stop and get your bearings before starting over again. Did you think a map or satellite navigation system would have been very useful to you at that point in time?

That's what it feels like when we try to navigate through life without understanding that there are various laws of nature to abide by in order to make the best of, and to enjoy, this life.

You now have a chance to get some bearings.

Fundamental Principles

Ideally, the custodian-observer should take the best care possible of BOTH the physical hardware and subtle software aspects.

This includes body and mind, heart, and nature.

Regarding laws and principles, we know that depending on where the humangee is born, and into what tradition, the paradigm of their laws may differ. There are literally hundreds of laws in some traditions. Many of these were established thousands of years ago at times when the world was much different.

However, there are commonalities in the foundations of most philosophic studies, writings, and religions. Through much analysis, we know these to be true.

Universal (Internal) Laws: The Roots of the Tree

You can liken these universal laws to a very deep root of a tree buried underground, which the ordinary eye cannot see, and yet the root exerts enormous influence on the tree. Without the root, the tree cannot withstand future strong winds.

The laws are interdependent. Events and situations often have multiple aspects that are thus influenced by multiple principles or laws. As a result, whether we are truly awake or not, we get to experience these laws at work each day. Most humangee do not see beyond the surface events to what is operating at this level.

Regarding daily activities and events, sometimes the outcomes of our actions work in our favor. However, when we have not aligned to these true principles, much to our surprise or irritation, they do not result in the outcomes we desire. There are consequences for not abiding by the laws. Ignorance or unawareness of these laws does not preclude them from operating.

Appreciate the Foundation of Humangee Life

There are numerous laws that have been articulated by philosophers, spiritual leaders, scientists, and others: think Hinduism's Wheel of Dharma, Buddhism's Noble Eightfold Path, the Five Pillars of Islam, and Christianity's Ten Commandments. The fundamental laws across these schools of thought are remarkably similar. They are not just guidance for a good life, they are also instructions toward inner harmony. More on this in chapter 5.

When we choose to ignore the natural laws, intentionally or unintentionally, we soon experience struggle, resistance, pain, and lack of direction. It inevitably leads to a sense of unfulfillment, lack of purpose, or some other equally life-sapping emotion.

As a society, we've evolved to believe mostly in the things we can see, feel, taste, hear, or touch while doubting anything beyond the perception of our five senses.

As a collective, we might have better technology, and we may have acquired

more knowledge of the physical world, but most of us do not see or understand these fundamental laws.

Hence, whether or not you believe in them, these universal laws influence our everyday lives. Much as we may like to, we cannot change that.

Seven Laws

As mentioned above, there are multiple views on how natural laws apply to humangee life.

This summary focuses on seven core laws or principles:

- Love
- Responsibility
- Unity
- Awareness – present moment
- Cause and Effect
- Essence
- Wisdom

The focus here is on mental laws and how they operate at the subtle, internal, and "software" level.

These laws are the bedrock on which our existence and the humangee operating system runs.

Assuming that we understand these, how do we make best use of that insight to manage our humangee to live a full and contented life?

The laws interoperate to establish and maintain proper working natural society. They are natural laws, like gravity and entropy.

They also apply to the full range of species and organisms on planet Earth.

These are laws of heart, mind, and universe—not just body. In our day-to-day physical body in human society, it is generally only the wrong actions of the body-device that are punished or deemed to be illegal or unjustified. Breaching laws in the physical world results in punishment in our physical society.

However, the natural law establishes that actions of mind and heart are of equal and often greater consequence. Breaching these eternal, intrinsic laws results in punishment in that internal mental world. At a minimum, we get a signal that there is something not right, which we generally ignore because we are not awake.

Our thoughts, actions, and words all carry weight and are either nurturing or undermining the humangee.

At this stage we will give a high-level overview of each of these internal-eternal laws.

For clarification, the term *internal* applies to the subtle being: mind, heart, nature,

and essence. *Eternal* refers to that which is permanent and lasts forever.

1. Love

In the study of wisdom, love is described as the natural cohering glue that impels all of the aspects of harmony, unity, responsibility, interoperation, cooperation, attention, awakeness, and dedication together. It is the singular primary emotion from which all other emotions emanate. It is the balancing force with discipline, with knowledge, with freedom. It allows many of the other aspects of our being to work in balance. What we are referring to is true, unlimited, unconditional, permanent love that extends to all. It is not limited to a small group and certainly not just to one being. It is described in more detail in chapter 14.

2. Responsibility

The central tenet here is that we are on this planet, in this universe, together. And while we may think that the world revolves around us alone, it revolves around everyone else too. You must understand who and what you are, and thus appreciate what your responsibilities are to yourself, your fellow humangee, other species, the Earth, and the cosmos. Delegation or abdication of responsibility comes at a price. More on this in chapter 13.

3. Unity

Unity is the state or quality of multiple attributes naturally joined or interwoven to form a single whole.

In the context of humangee and its internal and external environments, this law of unity reflects a natural operation in unison. It is helpful to see the planet and ecosphere as unified, inextricable ecosystems, where plants and animals (including humans) are unified by ancestry and are also part of the unified closed system. All are working as one.

Think of bees in the garden pollinating flowers: they are a vital part of that ecosystem. Each has an essential role to play that affects the collective. The bees intuitively know what part to play. The question is, have humangee so lost their contact with nature that they no longer fully understand why they are here and what role they serve in the play?

The inextricable link between humangee, Earth, plants, and all species in our unified ecosystem is also considered in the design principles section. It is validated by scientific analysis and connects the dots across the various disciplines. The links and dependencies between plants and insects are obvious: the symbiosis of plants breathing in carbon dioxide and putting out oxygen while their complementary animal species breathe in that oxygen and exhale CO_2. The whole process of evolution demonstrates literally thousands of examples of this interdependency.

The human product as an output of nature, overviewed in chapter 3 set out that the human species is simply a microcosm of the universe. The same rules of organism, evolution, and governing laws apply. The humangee software is a further microcosm of the same design. Hence it is little surprise that we find in practice that the outer world of the humangee reflects its inner world. This has significant repercussions, which we'll discuss in more detail at the end of chapter 5.

4. Awareness

Awareness determines the extent to which the humangee life is fully and properly experienced and lived—in its true state: **It reflects the capacity of the individual to be awake in the present moment.**

The present moment and awareness, when both properly understood, are essentially interchangeable.

The law of awareness states that if there is no awareness, there is no internal peace (smooth, refined mental operation making full and positive use of capabilities). And the extent of the awareness determines the extent of the peace.

Additionally, the performance, quality, and refinement of a task is maximized when humangee bring full awareness and attention. The opposite also applies. Bringing a low level of attention and unawareness to a task produces suboptimal results.

Like all the other humangee mental software laws, if true awareness is observed and positively acted on, the outcome is good. If it is unknown or not acted on, if the being is consistently in a dream state (not aware), there are other painful consequences. Ignorance of the law fits in this latter category.

True awareness operates without preference or judgment. More on this in chapter 9.

Eternal laws help establish clear direction

5. Cause and Effect

In terms of the humangee device, every input generates a record or a file. Whether we like it or not, these files ultimately generate an output. In effect, every thought, word, or deed is a seed. And at some stage these seeds will manifest into an output file—an action or outcome.

Hence, in the application-output sense, meaning consequences, we reap what we sow.

We also know that:

- Firstly, humangee don't really know or understand the law. If they did, they would reflect on the consequences of their choices, decisions, and actions, realizing the wider and longer-term impacts.
- And secondly, the humangee perception of time between input (cause) and output (effect) is not well understood or appreciated. There is a tendency to expect to see results quickly. But the full outcome happens in line with nature, not when we want or expect it. It is often much longer.

The law of cause and effect seems basic and straightforward, but how it shows up in our daily lives is hugely varied and warrants assessing on a case-by-case basis.

6. Essence

This is an important concept that may or may not resonate or make sense initially. So the request is just to keep an open mind to consider it.

Each human being is animated by a life force. It can be known as life force, soul, spirit, essence, or other names.

In this regard, all humangee are the same: every humangee has an essence.

This is its secret sauce, over and above the body-device, mind, and heart, allocated when a life was issued.

While all humangee are equal in terms of essence, the function, form, and physical and external characteristics or aspects for each vary based on the body, mind, heart, allocation, and environment they have been apportioned.

All humangee are equal, but their form, function, and roles differ.

So, our role is to see and appreciate the essence in our fellow humangee and act in accordance with that principle.

In essence, this view demands that we recognize our brothers and sisters on this planet as being the same as us. And, ideally, we aim to serve for collective good.

This life force leaves the body-vehicle when the body expires.

At their core, all humangee are pure, perfect, and complete in their natural form. This includes the humangee essence. *This assertion is fundamental and important and is therefore worth challenging or testing robustly.*

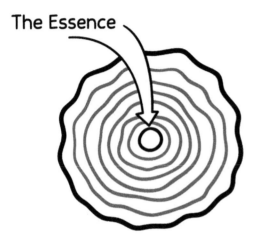

The Essence

The humangee essence is pure, perfect, and complete, but not visible or experienced due to being covered by many layers of opinions, beliefs, and misconceptions.

7. Wisdom

Eternal laws are essentially the system of rules that regulate and support humangee. They operate as a self-sustaining, self-regulating mechanism and apply across our world.

To philosophical thinkers, *wisdom* is the love of truth. It is associated with attributes such as compassion; detachment; ethical, benevolent, and unbiased judgment; humility; charity; experiential self-knowledge; self-transcendence. It is regarded as one of the highest virtues across religions and philosophy. It both illumines the mind and instills an attraction to the divine.

Wisdom encompasses a person with self-awareness as the one who witnesses the entire creation in all its facets and forms. Further, it reflects a level of realization that an individual through right conduct and right living, over an unspecified period, comes to realize their true relationship with our universe. It is central to most religions and is considered a state of mind and soul where a person achieves liberation.

In the context of humangee, wisdom is both a characteristic *and* a set of guiding principles. Love of learning about the truth is analogous to wisdom. To practice that wisdom in daily life with vigor is the aim.

In the context of the instruments that we discuss in this manual, there is a subtle distinction between wisdom and understanding, which Shane Mulhall reminded his philosophy students: understanding is a view taken by the mind, while wisdom is an experience undergone by the heart; one is light, the other love, and so they unite and complete one another.

With regard to wisdom, Buddha taught his students the threefold training of turning:

- greed into generosity and discipline,
- anger into kindness and meditation,
- ignorance into wisdom.

Further Guidelines

When one goes into detail on the implications of each of the laws described, there are a range of other more specific guidelines that emerge. A sample of these is covered below. These are by no means exhaustive, but give a flavor of the effects. They can be categorized in different ways.

Sample Daily Living—Universal Guidelines

1. **No desire to steal.** A truthful, aligned humangee earns his or her own way with honesty, hard work, and fairness. Hence, s/he does not countenance theft of objects but refrains from exploiting and depriving others of what is theirs, whether it is possessions, rights, or perspectives.

2. **Non-Violence.** A positive and dynamic force that prioritizes love, goodwill, benevolence, and tolerance of all living creatures.

3. **Truth.** The principle that equates unity with soul. It is the mainstay of the basic moral laws: one should be truthful—not act fraudulently, be dishonest, or lie in life. Truth is consistent with our essence and is fundamental to alignment of core aspects of our being.

4. **Non-Possessiveness.** Guides the humangee to live simply, to keep only those material things that are required to sustain the demands of daily life. According to some, the excessive hoarding and deprivation of assets and resources from others is tantamount to theft. This again needs to be properly understood in context.

5. **Cleanliness.** Respect for the internal and external aspects of both body and mind as well as the need to clean, refine, and maintain. The old adage goes: As within, so without. Your outside reflects your inside and vice versa. This truth aligns with the Buddhist philosophy of repair, reuse, and non-waste.

6. **Contentment.** Alertness to and conscious reduction of desires and identification. It reflects the limiting of ego-driven attainments, attachments, and possessions. (It does not preclude ambition, achievement, and success, but these need to be properly understood.)

7. **Good Company.** A collective term used for investing time and commitment to enable exposure to quality content and to use it to create an objective, unbiased, and pure mind. This may include the reading of quality material, use of podcasts or appropriate audio or video content. This enables the self-reflection required for clarity, alignment, and purity of one's own thoughts, acts, and deeds. It includes the study and interaction with like-minded people who are also on the journey to use their device properly.

8. **Discipline.** This can be thought of as asceticism, the performance of physical and mental discipline throughout a life of perseverance, focus, dedication, and even delayed gratification. The end objective is inner transformation. Humangee can still have a level of awakening while experiencing awake, happy, joyful living in our concrete jungles and normal lives. Hence, this discipline and focus can be satisfying, inspiring, and rewarding—it doesn't necessarily have to be all struggle and pain. For the current humangee device in the modern world, the stereotypical view of asceticism as the monastic, removed, and robed lifestyle is still an option, but it's somewhat outdated. The non-monastic approach of the householder is equally appropriate and

deemed to be needed more in today's society.

9. **Regular Dedication.** The humangee should perform every act in a selfless, detached, attentive, and natural way, where dedication to a unity or greater good is practiced. This removes the focus from me, mine, and ego and projects it outward for all. We can then accept the results of our deeds because we are not emotionally attached to the outcome, whether good or bad.

It is also a practice of most mainstream religions.

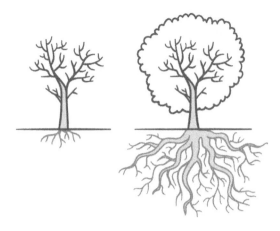

In a season of harvest, you reap what you sow

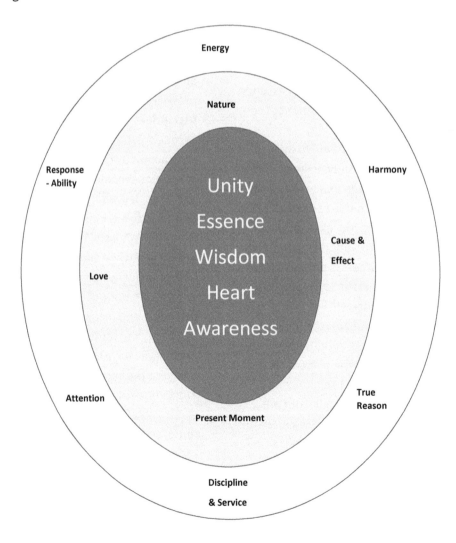

Conclusion

The daily life and work of aligning with these principles is generally unseen and uncredited (no need for likes, forwards, or kudos) and ideally proceeds without undue attachment to the result.

A joyful existence unfolds at the speed of life—not necessarily in the timeframe we want or desire it to.

The purpose of this diagram on the previous page is primarily to reflect that all of these aspects operate within the universe, in life on Earth, and within humangee. When humangee ignores one or more aspects, dissonance and friction occur. This may not seem obvious at the time, but it has long-term consequences and effects.

The Play: All the World's a Stage

The play is a useful model humangee can use to become fully alive and enjoy life.

In short, life is a play. All humangee are invited to participate and there are a wide range of roles, but you don't get a choice about which you play. You get a character, a body, a costume, an overview of your initial part, and the location in which your part of the production takes place.

You can have multiple functions within the play, but the primary three are onstage, backstage, and in the audience.

The same role can be viewed from onstage (i.e., from within the play) or from the audience (i.e., from outside the play).

With practice, you can even consciously switch perspectives. The benefit of

this is you get to be in the play (player) and watch as the custodian-observer (audience).

The scene is set, the play begins. The players perform their parts in each scene. As the play unfolds, it is invariably a mix of comedy, tragedy, humor, love, stress, excitement, anger, trials and tribulations, failure, and success. It's a real emotional roller coaster, passionate and full of drama, and true to life. It is life.

For the humangee, being in the play can be very intense, and it's often physically draining. The participation is fraught with a range of emotions,

Life in the play

reactions, events, challenges, problems, pleasures, and pain, often leaving the player physically and mentally exhausted after a few scenes.

The observer in the audience simply watches the interactions, players, and events, with enjoyment and detachment. This doesn't mean there is no compassion or empathy for what the players are experiencing, but there is a much lower level of attachment. Consequently, the play is enjoyed in full.

As far as I know, refreshments are served in the breaks also. Tickets for the play are not expensive but are only offered to those who are at least a little bit awake. ☺

A useful observation is that many of the players become so engrossed in their own parts that they forget the opportunity to step off, backstage, where they can be refreshed, gather themselves, check their lines, take a rest, and change their costume. They miss the opportunity to ⏸ (pause) properly so that when they do go back out, they are invigorated and ready for the next part. They also forget that it is from backstage that they can change and rejoin the audience, and thus enjoy the play from there.

This Is Important

This play is similar to humangee life in general. Whether we know it not, we are the stars of our own show, or participants in our localized play.

Pause from time to time and go backstage to have a look. With regular practice, you can observe, reassess, be present, wash, relax, reflect on the last scene, and rest appropriately before going back out.

The next time you come backstage, take the chance to come out to the audience and watch for a while from there.

You may be surprised at how much more you see, what you experience, and your capacity to really enjoy the play. And the play will only gain as a result.

More about the Custodian

Owner, observer, custodian—what's the relationship with humangee?

When asking "Who am I?" on reasonable analysis and reflection, a custodian may realize he or she is more than body, mind, and heart. We also know that as beings, we are able to observe our humangee; we're responsible for looking after it.

When fully awake, we can observe ourselves with some clarity. Depending on the context, the terms have different connotations. One that is relevant in the early stages of this manual is *custodian-observer*. But this is quite long-winded.

A useful initial term to describe the relationship with humangee is custodian. A *custodian* is responsible for taking care of or protecting something. It is also the term given to a person employed to clean or maintain a building or entity.

It aligns with one of the core philosophic teachings: "I am not this body; it is an instrument for my use."

This is consistent with what we observe as a conscious, awake, and present living individual.

When we learn to embed into our daily activities that we are a custodian for this body, mind, and heart, we start to appreciate our responsibility from a different perspective. It allows a form of detachment and freedom and enables us to see the component aspects of our mind a bit more objectively.

Before awakening, humangee don't realize that they have (and are) a custodian-observer, that it's a fundamental component of who and what they are. Consequently, believing that they are only body and mind, they are subject to all the trials and tribulations associated directly with the physical body and poorly managed mind. They believe that they are their ego, they experience attachment to ideas and things with few if any filters. They take life, events, and people too seriously. Hence, life is an uncontrollable emotional roller coaster. And the level of contentment and bliss is generally quite low. With the normal mindset, there is a focus on the external, extrinsic aspects of life.

However, when humangee begin to awaken and understand, appreciate, and embrace that, at its core, there is a custodian or observer for this device, then life changes.

The custodian-observer knows innately the fundamental rules and can understand how the mind works. From this perspective, they can better align with nature. And they are then in a position to listen to their heart and gut, to pay attention to and address the error signals that emerge. The custodian-observer can access and leverage the internal, intrinsic aspects.

It sounds easy—and it can be—but it does require a paradigm shift. This is important because if humangee can achieve this state, they are on to the next stage of the journey. It's a bit like mastering and progressing past a particularly difficult level in your favorite electronic game.

Day-to-day Reality

To make this shift, one must learn to be present more of the time. There are many distractions, resistance in some areas, and habits to undo or change. This work requires discipline and focus over time. Consequently, it is helpful if one finds others who are in the same process and can see the world from the same viewpoint.

Humangee may face ridicule and uncertainty as they awaken to this state. That's why it so important to get the foundation investigation and understanding correct. The path can be lonely for a period, but that changes to contentment with time and practice.

So, at this stage, the main term we will use is custodian-observer, custodian for short.

> We will find as time progresses that the true relationship is simply an observer. But the custodian-observer model serves as a useful stepping stone in the interim. The two terms will be used together and interchangeably from here on.

Eternal Laws
Love, Responsibility, Unity,
Presnt Moment, Cause &
Effect, Essence, Wisdom

**Eternal laws are the foundation
for other aspects of mind**

Chapter 5
BIOCHA Bunnito: Religion, Spirituality, and Other Considerations

Humangee, Practical Philosophy, and Religion

Let's consider the relationship between practical philosophy and religion and their importance to one another. In simplistic terms, religion may be favored by those who like to worship while philosophy may be favored by those who like to know. Religion is the search for God through faith, while philosophy is the search for truth through observation. Ultimately, we may find that God and truth are two aspects of the same unity. Is it possible that religion and philosophy may in some way complement each other? Without philosophical rigor, religion might be oriented as superstition and faith-dependent while philosophy without devotion or some aspect of divinity could be seen as incomplete or an intellectual, nonpractical pursuit.

> **What we do know is that the religions of the world share key observations and core principles about morality and guidelines for living.**

Reflecting on the last few millennia, you can see that the spread and evolution of various religions is a bit like a game of Telephone. In Telephone, a message is whispered from one person to another down the line of players until the final person relays the message as they received it, which is often radically changed from the original message. The real-world version of this game results in information being passed on from generation to generation, becoming significantly distorted over time.

For example, imagine a group of friends are traveling together to a faraway place. On their return, they reflect on some events from their trip, sharing statements or stories with different people. Not all the travelers had the same experience, observation, or interpretation, and thus the perceptions are different. All participants put their own twist on the stories, meals, and interactions, passing on the interpretations over time to different people and in hugely varied environments. Continue this over thousands of years, and you end up with a colorful spectrum of views and explanations from the single original event.

The purpose of this overview is to demonstrate that further assessment of any maker or source is unnecessary for the moment. We have enough of the "life on Earth" laws and fundamentals to work with.

Common Ground

The summary below provides an overview of the main religions of the world. The underlying consistency between them is uncanny. Thus it is helpful to focus on and appreciate their similarities rather than their differences.

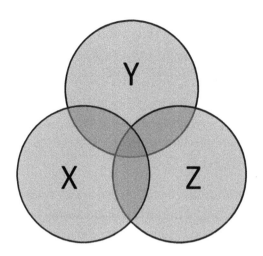

We can choose to focus on what we have in common

BIOCHA Bunnito

This is simply an acronym for the collective religions or beliefs: Buddhism, Islam, Others, Christianity, Hinduism, and Atheism—**but not necessarily in that order.**

All or most of the religions take the word and teachings of a great leader or prophet and collate, distill, and pass on their messages and recommendations. Leaders and prophets like Muhammad, Christ, Buddha, and others were role models whose actions, words, and demeanor provided clear and unambiguous direction.

In addition to the similarities in fundamental principles and laws, as put forward by the founders, there are numerous similarities in the way the laws and recommendations are implemented and promulgated.

These include the following recommendations:

1. Practice stillness, reflection, and prayer
2. Prioritize selflessness and consideration for the wider group (and ultimately fellow humangee)
3. Understand the need for constant vigilance, lest bad thoughts and habits take root like weeds in the mind-garden
4. Do not steal or covet
5. Take a single mindful day per week
6. Honor thy father, thy mother, and children
7. Do not kill/murder
8. Love your neighbor as yourself
9. Do not lie or swear falsely
10. Dedicate your efforts to something greater than yourself
11. Practice charity

The full range of laws and rules is extensive and remains the focus of debate about their true meaning.

The following overview is for background only and can be skipped as appropriate.

A High-Level Overview of the Main Religions on Earth

Around 6.5 billion people around the world follow some type of religious belief, while nearly 1.2 billion have no religious belief.

The purpose of this section is to convey that all humangee have much in common, regardless of their religious affiliation.

Not all humangee whose custodian ascribes to a specific religion actually fully embrace and truly live that system of beliefs and rules as intended. So you may read "followers" in the next section to mean apparent followers.

⏸ ▶ ■

Christianity: 2.4 billion followers in total. There are multiple Christian denominations within the three main branches: Catholicism, Protestantism, and Orthodox. It is one of three Abrahamic religions and is based on the teachings of Jesus Christ.

Islam: 1.8 billion followers. Originated in Mecca or Medina. Islam started sometime in the seventh century during the life of the prophet Muhammad, who is believed to be the last prophet of Allah. It's one of the Abrahamic religions. Hence it shares many similarities with Christianity and Judaism. The holy book of Islam is known as the Quran, and there are two main branches of Islam: Sunni and Shia.

Hinduism: at 1.1 billion followers, it is the largest religion in India. Differing from the other two world-leading religions, Hinduism is polytheistic, and thus its followers believe in many gods. Hindus have been practicing in one form or another for more than 4,000 years. The major scriptures are the Vedas and Upanishads, the Bhagavad Gita, the Ramayana, and the Āgamas. Hindus believe in:

- Dharma (ethics/duties)
- Artha (prosperity/work)
- Kama (desires/passions)
- Moksha (liberation/freedom from the cycle of death and rebirth/salvation)
- Karma (action, intent, and consequences)
- Saṃsāra (cycle of death and rebirth)

Buddhism: 500 million followers. Based on the teachings of Siddhartha Gautama. Branches of Buddhism include Theravada Buddhism and Mahayana Buddhism.

While Buddhism is generally categorized as a religion, the founder reiterated that it is not a religion but a way of life. There is no central God in the Buddhist belief.

Buddhism shares many similarities with Hinduism and follows the Wheel of Dharma, which is the eightfold path to live a righteous life.

Shintoism: 104 million followers. Dates back to the eighth century. It is well established in Japanese society and daily life, and has a form of religious modesty where a follower doesn't necessarily declare their faith publicly.

Sikhism: 30 million followers. A younger religion thought to have originated in the fifteenth century. Many Sikhs are recognized by their turbans.

Judaism: 15 million followers. The oldest of the Abrahamic religions.

There are three main branches of Judaism: Orthodox, Conservative, and Reform with various smaller sects that follow their own interpretation of the religion. The Jewish holy book is known as the Torah, and their religious laws can be found in the Talmud, which contains the 613 commandments of Moses, also known as the Mosaic law.

Taoism: 12 million followers. Also known as Daoism, it developed around 2,000 years ago in China. Laozi is thought to have written the Tao Te Ching (the central text of Taoism) and is considered to be the founder. A further 90 million are known to join Taoism activities.

Korean Shamanism: 10 million followers. Also known as Muism, this belief system has several deities and spirits. The practice of Muism dates back to prehistoric times before Confucianism and Buddhism were introduced.

Confucianism: 6 million followers. This religion is based on the teachings of Confucius:

Five virtues within Confucianism:

- Jen (goodwill, empathy, generosity)
- Yi (rightness, duty as guardians of nature and humanity)
- Li (right conduct and propriety, demonstrating your inner attitude with your outward expressions)
- Chih (wisdom)
- Hsin (faithfulness and trustworthiness)

Caodaism: 4.4 million followers. Cao Dai is a belief system in Vietnam, founded by Ngo Van Chieu in 1926. It's essentially a mix of aspects from the larger religions with the belief in one Supreme Being and placing great emphasis on peace, love, tolerance, and justice.

There are another 4,000+ religions across the world.

Atheism is the absence of religious belief, claimed by around 800 million people and is a growing trend in many countries.

> *How is it possible that a being with such sensitive jewels as the eyes, such enchanted musical instruments as the ears, and such fabulous arabesque of nerves as the brain can experience itself anything less than a god?*
>
> Alan Watts, Philosopher

Hmg Essence

Guidelines Are Sufficiently Generic and Applicable to All

Advaita Vedanta philosophy, which is essentially a distillation of truths from numerous other teachings, offers a simple open-minded perspective, concluding that, if there is a God or other single source or entity, then there is probably only one of them, not one for each religion or belief system.

For the purposes of this book, we focus on the universe and the unity of all things, as well as practical aspects we can experience through our observations in daily life.

Hence this set of guidelines for humangee should be largely aligned with ALL of these belief systems where the core principles are in essence the same.

Current Humangee Education and Training in the Nature of the Instrument

Humangee go to school with the intention of parents and our society to "get an education." Humangee travel to and from school, meet other kids, play in the playground, make friends, enjoy some things, dislike others. They are provided the opportunity to learn what is needed to pass a range of benchmark tests. These include formal academic assessments at every level of education.

Particularly in Western cultures, much of the teaching relates to the accumulation of historical facts and ultimately the passing of a state exam.

Many cultures place little focus on understanding the underlying philosophy, insight and life values, messages, tools, and skills to be passed on. Students gain little guidance in distinguishing between intrinsic and extrinsic attention. Few learn and ingrain the habit of stillness, presence, and awakeness (see chapter 9).

Historically, schools expected that this values-focused learning was supplemented outside of school—at home, in church, or through religious, tribal, or community groups. That is becoming less common with the passing of time.

Hence the current humangee may get some religious instruction, but s/he misses out on understanding the foundational principles and practices that were once instilled and reinforced over time.

So, what process should or could inspire an understanding of true principles for the humangee? Hopefully, we will see in the coming chapters.

Religion and Science Domination

The appreciation and acceptance of nature and natural principles was foundational to human existence until the advent of religious beliefs and doctrine and its associated crusades. It led dominant nations to see those nations with divergent religious beliefs as being inferior. Subsequently, religion dominated as a mechanism for control in many countries—to the extent that heathens, pagans, or infidels were despised and often tortured. Over centuries the scientific, literary, and other communities had to be careful. It was only after Copernicus and others in the 1500s that the sciences gained acceptance as being of value. With the Industrial Revolution, science took on a much stronger position. It emerged as a new mechanism for domination and international leadership. It has progressed over the last two hundred years and brought us to the present time, in an age sometimes described as scientific materialism. Scientific development has been effective in some areas and less so in others. There are incomplete insights across numerous disciplines from biology, chemistry, natural sciences, and physics. Science is beginning to acknowledge a sparsely understood middle ground in energy, matter, biological systems, and the quantum realm.

Sage and Scientist Meet at Unity

Let's consider how the concept of source or unity has been approached in the past and examine some conclusions reached by humankind over the years.

Aristotle was credited with two areas of work:

- **Physics:** which addressed natural philosophy, what we call science today, and
- **Metaphysics:** which dealt with questions about the reality beyond what we perceive with our senses.

The physics aspects have become mainstream, taught in schools around the world. Metaphysics is a less popular field of study because it needs to be experienced to be validated. Physics can be more easily explained, since it studies the properties of the material world (e.g., sound, heat, weight, speed, light, etc.).

We will use a few aspects to convey the parallel but separate views of each approach.

The metaphysics approach led to three groundbreaking discoveries:

- Since the body, mind, and nature are all known (i.e., there is a knower), they cannot be ultimate.
- The known is always changing: things, plants, people, thoughts. Thus, it cannot be ultimate.
- That which knows the changeable must know the unchangeable: Could you have a knower, who does not know? (No)
- Hence, it's unlikely that one could have a knower that is not conscious.

- In metaphysics, the determinant of whether something is real or true is if it is immutable—not subject to change.

The physics approach, over a more recent time period, has made similar revelations: Einstein and his colleagues spent even more time on a unifying theory than on the theory of relativity. Relativity essentially explained physics at a macroscopic level, where Niels Bohr's theory of quantum mechanics explained physics at the microscopic level.

Both physics areas have concluded a unifying theory, a four-dimensional concept called space-time, but as yet have been unable to prove it. In the same way that earlier research concluded that energy and mass were not separate things—just different manifestations of the same thing—they concluded that the assumptions behind the current paradigm of space and time were flawed.

Einstein and many leaders in the physics community believed and proposed that there should be some unifying general principles by which we could construct a consistent, functioning universe. Essentially, if we probed deeply enough, we would discover one and only one way in which all the components—matter, radiation, forces, space, and time—would fit together to make reality work, just as the gears, springs, dials, and wheels of a mechanical clock uniquely combine to track time.

Professor David Bohm advanced this idea in his theory of the implicate order, which came to the highly probable conclusion that the material world is part of a single totality. This has been further progressed and increased in complexity by the use of quantum theory, and string or M-theory, which resorts to high levels of probability rather than definitive provable conclusions. It does however continue to validate the essential interconnectedness of the universe. (Again, a case of we know that it works but we're not sure how.)

Dr. David Bohm has been a leading figure in this area. Einstein referred to him as his spiritual son, and the Dalai Lama named him as his physics and science guru. He fits into the unicorn category of a true scientist-sage.

Both physics and metaphysics approaches end up pointing to a conclusion of the unified field, but from two different directions.

Within human or humangee life, we could refer to this tendency toward unity as a unifying drive. And we can link this to practical experience and existing insight.

The *unifying drive* is consistent with the themes conveyed in this manual: the unity in nature, where everything is interconnected and part of the whole. A consistent set of laws and principles applies.

Beyond the basic survival needs, humangee displays three clear primordial qualities, which underpin everything in human life and its aspirations.

- Knowledge: to seek and know the truth
- Consciousness: to live a full life as an awake being
- Bliss: to be happy

These will be explored in more detail in section 2.

In this manual, we seek to pare back our view of the world to the bare essentials, enabling reality and truth to be seen without all the usual "noise."

Practical Philosopher-Sage	Scientist
Metaphysics approach	Physics approach
Focuses on the knower (Observer)	Focuses on the known (Object)
Attention focused inward	Attention focused outward (via senses)
Toward increasing simplicity	Toward increasing complexity
Intuitive aspect of mind	Thinking aspect of mind
Conclusion: The unified field – acknowledged and agreed	**Conclusion:** The unified field – acknowledged and widely agreed
Tools: Surrender, insight, meditation, stillness, observation	**Tools:** Theory, assumptions, analysis, calculation, measure
Plato, Descartes, and Philosopher-Sage inquirers	Einstein, Tesla, Bohm, others

The Significance of Unity and Universe

The relevance of this science–philosophy overview is simply to demonstrate the fact that we can approach key questions from the direction of increasing complexity (science) or increasing simplicity (practical philosophy).

Investigations of areas in the external, known, physical world, like mathematics, physics, biology, chemistry, Earth and nature, and philosophy, can ultimately be simplified to a small set of unifying fundamentals, or ultimately toward a unity.

This theme and observation continue when we consider the analysis of the mental and internal laws and foundations, components, or aspects and their interactions.

The same logic and processes that we can see and demonstrate externally, we can now observe internally (at a software/mind level), albeit to a less tangible extent.

Chapter 6

Operating System and Applications

Many humangee give little thought to aspects of their being beyond their body. Most are under-aware of the vital mind-body link. The control operations that function between the two parts are such that you cannot affect one without affecting the other.

Ego | Discursive mind

Operating system overview

True reason | Heart

Energy states

Eternal Laws

Humangee mind components overview diagram

Operation System Overview

The core operating system overview diagram shows the principal aspects of mind and how they work together. It's also useful for clarifying distinctions between natural operation of mind and incorrect or unnatural use. There are three key layers:

1. Eternal laws, which are the foundation
2. Energy states, which affect operation of the mind
3. Aspects of mind and the interoperation of these key functions

Collectively, they determine the operation of the mind and ultimately the operation

of humangee. The capacity to manage the device most efficiently requires that the custodian have a basic understanding of the components and how to operate the process properly. This may be innate or acquired.

The aspects will be explained in more detail as we progress.

We know from the earlier description that the hardware and the interfaces of eyes, ears, skin, mouth, nose, and senses remain largely constant. These are like the input devices on a cell phone: screen interface, touch activation, keyboard, video camera, microphone, Siri/Alexa, and internal orientation capabilities. These provide feeds into the associated applications, which work autonomously and are largely taken for granted.

From an operating system and software perspective, the design, performance, and security aspects are sound, but most users are simply not aware of the applications, proper management, and use of the device.

Aspects of the Mind Operating System

There are some aspects of the humangee mind that are important but are misinterpreted, made overly complicated, or not generally talked about. We will spend a bit of time describing these.

When understood, these distinctions enable observation, understanding, management, and enjoyment of your device.

1. Eternal Laws, as overviewed in chapter 4.
2. Energy States

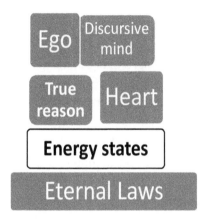

There are three basic energy states, which we describe as:

- Fervent
- Dull
- Awake

These relate to the frame of mind and associated nature of the energy in each state. These reflect the type of energy present in a humangee at a particular point in time and are described in later chapters in more detail.

The Fervent State: Humangee is busy or active and possibly focused on activities or work, pushing hard to get things done. Energy level is high and the being is enthusiastic, energetic, driven, and in some cases agitated. In its extreme, it can be too rushed and insensitive.

The Dull State: Humangee is slow-moving and appears to lack energy or enthusiasm. This is useful when slowing down to go to

sleep or in the latter winding-down stages of a natural cycle. It's not helpful in an environment where focus, clarity, and activity are needed. It is useful from a regulation and timing efficiency perspective. In its extreme, it could convey laziness or sloth.

The Awake State: This is generally the preferred state for humangee, in which the being is fully awake and alert. The head is clear and attention is centered or open. This is also when best work and interactions are had.

All energies are present in the being, but one or two tend to dominate at a particular time. And some individuals can have strong tendencies toward one or another for more of the time.

❚❚

3. Four Aspects of Mind

Consider the analogy of a laptop device. If we didn't have the concepts of operating systems, applications, hardware, software, data, storage, settings, access, and users, we would not have the lexicon to fully articulate how different aspects work together. So the systematic development of a collectively agreed terminology has allowed the technology area to flourish. We have common language and interpretation that all players in the market know and understand. From that foundation we can work collectively and agree on refinements in each area and devise solutions to problems at a component level as well as a user and application level.

In the same way, the base terminology outlined here is to help humangee custodians describe how the component parts of the mind operate. Collectively, they demonstrate the nature of functions that certain aspects deliver and consequently help explain the interactions that take place. These aspects are so fundamental to the operation of the mind of a humangee that if they are not clearly understood, you will not truly learn how to understand your device and allow it to work for you.

There are four aspects of mind:

a. Discursive mind
b. True reason/Faculty of reason
c. Heart/Emotional Gut
d. Ego

These aspects are discussed extensively in Vedic philosophies under their original Sanskrit names.

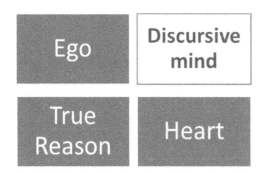

a. The Discursive Mind is connected with all the senses and receives information and impressions from them, as well as generating its own from other internal stimuli. On the basis of these inputs, it is then responsible for churning out thoughts and ideas that pertain to the stimulus. It is an exceptionally active, proficient, and thorough component. It literally generates tens of thousands of thoughts and ideas every day. We only actually register a percentage of these; most go unnoticed by the conscious mind.

When presented with a problem, the discursive mind has a capacity to look at it from many angles and generate ideas and options. These problems, queries, and considerations can span a spectrum from good to bad, founded to unfounded, and relevant to irrelevant.

It is a key aspect of human creativity, problem solving, and original and inventive thinking. However, it is potentially the most destructive component of our inner-mind instrument that we need to understand and be able to observe. If we don't, it generates an unending supply of thoughts and ideas; if unmanaged, they can take on a life of their own. Rogue programs, applications, and habits can start to develop. While some of these can be positive, many of them don't run in alignment with the natural laws. So, vigilance and maintenance are vitally important.

It's a bit like breathing, it continues since you are alive. The discursive mind operates that way. There will be a constant stream of thoughts, but you have much more scope to understand and direct them if you are awake and present and understand the device.

It's the part of mind that can keep you anxious or awake at night with constant thoughts. One of the skills to develop is the ability to observe and understand that these are just thoughts and do not necessarily require any attention, action, or attachment.

So, while the discursive mind can take inputs and generate these interpretations, ideas, and thoughts, that's where its capability stops. It can only generate thoughts;

it cannot conclude them. This function to assimilate and problem-solve is provided by the faculty of reason (or True Reason).

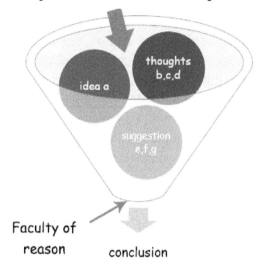

Discursive mind... generates a stream of thoughts

Faculty of reason   conclusion

b. True Reason (Faculty of Reason) is the faculty of mind that collates, reasons, and discriminates on the various inputs and insights. It operates best when the discursive mind has done its part and collected all the relevant information and is allowed to fall quiet.

If the humangee is not attached to the thoughts, and is properly awake, it can make a clear decision based on a combination of the natural laws, the other aspects of mind, and the information that has been provided. Cultivating stillness and allowing true reason to work enables clearer, sounder, better decisions.

The opposite also applies. If the mind continues to be active while making a decision, reason does not get the chance to operate. This results in poor quality decisions.

■■

c. The Heart (Emotional Gut) is what most would describe as heart. Not the physical one, but the one that forms the center of our emotional being, a hugely powerful component that links well with memory and recognition. It's the place where gut instinct and intuition come from. It is accessible only when humangee is in an awake or connected state, often with love in the heart. It is fundamental to motivation; it is what drives humangee.

■■

d. The Ego relates to who I think I am. One's ego generates attachment to things of the physical world.

No or low ego reflects low attachment. High ego reflects high attachment. Humangee should be guided by reason. And when too much focus is on wants rather than needs, on achievement of objectives without respect for consequences, or on excessive worldly goods or specific outcomes and things, the ego is strong. In this state, it can often veer toward being very selfish or egotistical.

It's not all bad, in that it gives drive and focus to the individual and helps them make changes. It can also be observed, managed, and refined or reduced over time.

It also relates to who I think I am relative to other people: superior, smarter, richer, better looking, more than in some way or another. It thus becomes judgmental. This should be avoided. And while there may be aspects where the visible daily role or function appears of a higher or lower level, humangee should focus on the essence in others and themselves whenever possible.

It is fully appreciated that humangee need to earn a living and often support a family. There is an opportunity to find the balance of being able to do this while still enjoying "the play of life" in the process.

These four aspects of mind are explored in detail in section 2.

Internal or External— Appreciation and Understanding

The device has aspects that primarily focus on:

- External: sense-oriented aspects, physical body and my world, my life.
- Internal: subtle, still, natural environment.

The physical external world environment is designed to be challenging. We know that life can be tough. It is populated with many humangee all with similar needs and wants.

The default setting for a humangee is to look to the external world, most likely originating from the physical survival instinct. However, when one has been awakened and better understands the internal workings, they have the opportunity to appreciate the wider laws and principles and distinguish between an externally and internally focused life, or strive for a better balance between the two.

With little appreciation of what their settings are configured to, humangee often go off track and increasingly seek pleasure, goods, and comforts, identifying with externally motivated desires.

❚❚

The Self-Correcting Function

Humangee's self-correcting function provides various forms of feedback. Your mind sends signals that you may be asleep or awake to.

These feedback signals are used to convey that something may not be aligned properly. For example, it might convey that harboring jealousy, anger, hurt, or worry, the pursuit of status or pleasures, do not support or nourish us mentally. The unawakened humangee is unaware, deaf, blind, and ignorant to these feedback signals.

The Two Wolves

We can use this story to reflect on the impact of the ego and desires, which can obscure what is natural and good.

There was a wise old lady talking with her humangee child. During their conversation one day, she recounted that in the old days, there was unhappiness within her.

"It was like a struggle between two sides—an internal, relentless fight between two wolves.

"The dark, evil one was greedy, egocentric, and self-centered, and was generally discontent. It held misery, anger, jealousy, arrogance, selfishness. It was also judgmental, lacked remorse, believed the world revolved around it and owed it something. It believed itself to be superior; it shifted guilt to others, was resentful, had self-pity, and lied to itself and others.

"The other was good, serene, humble, graceful, compassionate, and grateful. Thoughtful and considerate to others, it exuded joy and love. Truthful with self and others, it sought to serve all. It too could be firm and ferocious. The good wolf demonstrated equanimity, hope, focus, attention, empathy, kindness, and generosity in a way that was appropriate."

Which will win?

The same struggle occurs in most people, she explained, until they awaken and see or appreciate the natural laws and the impact they have in every aspect of our lives.

"In modern life, there is a view that some of the evil wolf characteristics are useful—to get ahead, make more money, or not be walked over, that we should focus single-mindedly on our personal goals and aspirations. This is not true.

"These types of actions have consequences, most of which are not good.

"When you understand these principles properly, you see that these negative characteristics don't serve you in the longer term.

"It's a bit like forming a bad habit—even if they produce a result in the short term, that may simply give a reward to reinforce their use. But the long-term impact is a joy-sapping journey downward. It is increasingly detrimental over time."

The child thought over everything she had heard. Finally, she asked, "Which wolf will win?"

The old lady replied, *"The one you feed."*

Humangee reaps the rewards of the characteristics that its custodian allows it to focus on.

We all have a choice about how we respond to events and circumstances. We have the opportunity to take responsibility for ourselves and choose our own path and our own freedom in how we make best use of the challenges that we are given to navigate.

 **Settings**

In the same way that your mobile phone has settings to control how messages are received and at what volume and within which time ranges they are issued, the human device has settings that may be regulated. Use the guide below to assess the device settings on your humangee.

Just like your mobile, some settings are simply on/off, others are on a sliding scale from Low (0%) to High (100%). It is useful to consider your default settings.

SETTINGS		
Aware of the play		✓
Committed to enjoy the play		✗ [1]
External/Internal aware - default ext.		Ext [2]
Attuned Listening	0 - 10	4 [3]
Attuned Perception	0 - 10	5 [4]
Respond (default- React- off X)		✓[5]
See the Play daily	0 - 10	3 [6]
Take self-responsibility	0 - 10	5 [7]
Receiving inputs filter	0 - 10	1 [8]
Talk/Listen – Ratio (<1 or >1) (>1 talks more than listens)		>1 [9]
Alarm & Error Options		🔕 [10]
Attention state awareness		ON

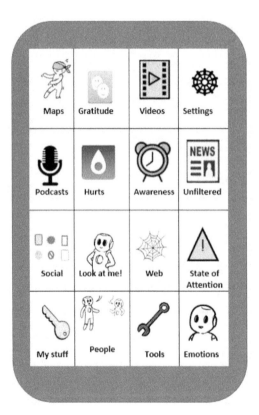

THIS INTERFACE IS NOT AVAILABLE IN CURRENT MODELS

Explanation Notes

[1] Numbers relate to the references in the mobile screen above.

[2] Awareness that we can also view humangee from a distance—be detached

[3] Ideally, we want to change this setting to also include an internal focus

[4] We listen actively, without passing judgment or planning how we will respond

[5] How awake and detached am I to what is going on around me?

[6] The preference is to respond as opposed to react

[7] Committed to participate in the play—with scope to raise the level of detachment

[8] See chapter 13

[9] Be conscious of what you let take hold in your mind (i.e., what you attach to)

[10] An awake humangee listens more than it talks

[11] Listens to error signals in body and mind

❚❚

Attention

Attention is one of the core master skills for humangee, particularly in the context of giving full attention to the task at hand.

Is the device multitasking or single-tasking?

Female humangee are credited with being natural multitaskers, while males are thought to need more practice. However, regardless of gender, each device is well capable of multitasking.

The humangee device has simultaneous input and output capabilities, including limbs, sense organs, and mental faculties, that can effectively operate at the same instant. Hence, one would expect that the processing capacity is simply diluted when spread across multiple activities. Multiple actions may be undertaken simultaneously like listening to the radio, preparing food, packing a bag to take to work, planning ahead for later in the day, scheduling an event for next month, while possibly carrying some irritation from an activity yesterday. The list could go on.

Superficially, the human can be rather effective at multi-tasking, and it is useful for getting a lot done in a short span of time. However, when the attention is divided, precision, attentiveness, and joy in the activity may be compromised.

One can address this on a case-by-case basis, and if attention is Open, marvel in the outstanding simultaneous, discreet processing and completion of tasks when done with love and efficiency.

❚❚ ▶ ■

Modes of Attention

The device operates at different modes of attention: There are four primary modes: See diagram below.

Open The device is fully awake and alert and tuned in to numerous multi-sensory activities occurring and happening around it.	**Captured** The device is in *locked* mode, purely focused on one activity or event, but in the asleep/non-awake state. Hence, they have reduced control of their outputs, thought processing, and resulting actions, like in a state of anger, fear, or dispondency.

Attention

Centered This is the most efficient state for productivity, creativity, and clarity. The device is still, fully awake, clearly focused with singular attention on the task at hand. In this state, optimal work is done, and the device experiences happiness and satisfaction. Time stands still, and the device is fully present.	**Scattered** The device is essentially in a dream state. There are many functions and operations being attended to by the device, but with reduced clarity or efficiency. Like a moving magnifying glass, it has limited effect. While some of the activities may be completed, there is no precision or happiness.

Open and Centered attention are optimal. These tend to occur when the being is present or in a state of awakeness and openness, and consequently yields a more contented state. Scattered and Captured are much less beneficial and effective—often detrimental. When your attention is captured and locked onto something, it is not properly conscious and is often incapable of seeing sense or reality. Consequently, it is in this state (e.g., rage) that humans do silly things that they regret later when the "red mist" of anger has settled. In simpler terms, humangee make mistakes in this state, resulting in a form of misery.

▌▌

Key Takeaways – regarding states of attention

- This relatively subtle concept has huge ramifications.
- How much of the time are we in each state?
- What is the most appropriate state— when at work, when with friends, when doing work at home, when in the car, when relaxing?
- Recommended state to be either Open or Centered.
- One should try to **reduce/avoid Scattered**.
- **Misery comes pre-packaged with Captured.**

The Happiness Decision Switch

Happiness Is a Simple Choice

When the humangee awakens and understands that happiness simply exists in the natural state, he or she can enjoy it any time, any place, literally at will. And, like the physical muscles, if it is exercised regularly, it grows and works for you.

If we were to put a value on happiness, what would it be? A month's income, a year's income, more? What's it worth to you?

We get opportunities every day to keep it. We allocate it no value. We spend all our savings taking the body on exotic holidays and buying it nice things, expecting to gain happiness. But like sleeping morons, we choose, day in and day out, to give away our happiness for free!

So, for those who have studied and observed the humangee device, the clear instruction is: appreciate the importance of not selling or giving away the happiness—not for anyone or anything at any time.

It's yours to have and to keep, by birthright. You can keep it, irrespective of the circumstance.

It is a choice and a discipline. For a more in-depth discussion of how to help your humangee cultivate happiness, see chapter 10.

Sleep: Self-Maintain Daily Reset Cycle

Most humangee have an appreciation of the rejuvenating and reinvigorating qualities of sleep. So much so, that it is a clear part of each humangee's daily routine.

Humangee require regular sleep, which provides a software and hardware recalibration and a low-impact reset. With the right support and management, your humangee is designed to start each and every day completely afresh, as a block of 16+ hours in which to serve you, other humangee, and the wider world.

In ideal conditions it might be given water at some stage before it goes into REST (Recalibration Enabling State Time) and should also have access to some when it wakens. It rejuvenates best on a relatively empty stomach.

Whenever possible, it is helpful if the waking-up process is natural and gentle. Apparently, there are some good apps for that also.

The humangee device likes and adapts well to natural cycles of dark and light. Hence exposure to artificial light from computers, phones, and other devices is not ideal during the wind-down period before it sleeps.

In warmer countries it is not uncommon for humangee to have a short REST (Recalibration Enabling-State Time). These are often taken during the warm part of the day or early afternoon.

In this state it has no desires and is completely happy.

Sleep =
- Recharge
- Reset
- Repair
- Realign

Live the laws and guidelines
- Understand the eternal laws and validate them in practice
- Understand the universal guidelines, actions, and practices
- Observe your current choices, reactions, and paradigms in practice
- Appreciate the consequences if you are not aligned with the laws and guidelines

Improve insight and practice
- Understand and manage energy states and aspects of mind
- Consider and assess your potential misconceptions (Ch 10)
- Establish changes and resets required
- Establish some helpful daily practices and routines
- Be present - mindfulness in all activities

Initial actions
- Decide to be happy - now
- Choose to let go of misery or attachment when it appears
- Observe and understand your ego – Who I think I am
- Pursue self-inquiry
- Enjoy the journey rather than focusing on the destination
- Learn to detach and observe yourself and the events of life

The Principal and the Dinner Lady

There once was a principal who was puzzled by some of the aspects taught in religion at the school. So she put a question to one of the teachers, "Where is God and what does he do?" The teacher was a bit uncertain. Just like the principal, he did not have a response but committed to ask around and let the principal know the answer.

The teacher was worried and uneasy with the question, so he discussed the problem with others in the cafeteria. He remembered one of the dinner ladies[3] who worked in the cafeteria was very wise. She was always active, happy, and satisfied, for she was in contact with a spiritual person by whom she had been initiated into true wisdom and reflection. He approached her, and she offered her services to assist the teacher. The teacher was at first apprehensive, but seeing the dinner lady's confidence and serenity, took her to see the principal.

The principal asked her the question. The dinner lady asked for a bowl full of milk, in which she moved her finger without

---

3 More commonly called lunch ladies in the US.

stopping. After a while, the impatient principal asked what she was doing, saying that the dinner lady was expected to answer the question, not just sit there and stir the milk with her finger. The dinner lady said that she was looking for butter in the milk. The principal said angrily, "No one can get butter out of milk the way you're trying to do it. You must go through a systematic process of churning it thoroughly. Only then will you see butter coming out of the milk."

The dinner lady said that was right and that it also applied to the principal's question about God. "To see and find God, one has to go through a systematic process, and only then is it possible to reach a stage where one can see God.

"This is the answer to the first question. Now unless there is a proper relationship between teacher and disciple, I do not intend to answer the next question, for it will not be of much use." The principal apologized for her outburst and became a follower and respecter of the dinner lady.

The purpose of this story is simply to highlight that there is a process to assist awakening. It starts with understanding the foundational principles. And then builds by addressing misconceptions and understanding the distinction of living in the present.

(Adapted from a story in conversations with Sri Shantananda Sarasvati)

Chapter 7
Data Storage, Accumulation, Archiving, and Access

Residual Data and Pre-Existing Programs

With most technological devices, the operating systems come pre-installed. This is true also for humangee. However, unlike a brand new PC, the humangee device also has the core applications installed, some pre-existing mini-programs, and some historical data. We have termed this old content or programming as *baggage*.

So, while identical twins may look the same from birth, they may have slightly different natures and display differences in their attitudes and behaviors. As a result of their individual baggage, some of the differences may be subtle and others not. Each has a pure, perfect, and complete essence.

Also, each humangee is born into a unique family, ethnic, community, religious, geographic, or demographic environment. So, in summary, we all start from differing places and with varying characteristics in our diverse environments.

Where did I come from?

Remember the play from chapter 4? When humangee are born, we are all allocated different roles in the play, and our opportunity is to play the part to the best of our ability. So, imagining you're in *Mary Poppins* (the movie or the play), it wouldn't matter whether you were a chimney sweep or a bank manager. Both participants have to deliver their part in full and are integral to the whole play. This is exactly the same for all humangee born into life.

Irrespective of the starting point, and the initial baggage and resources allocated, each humangee's primary commitment is to accept responsibility for the role they have been allocated, live by the laws and guidelines, do their best, and try and leave the planet a bit better than they found it—by whatever means they can. We'll explore this idea in more detail in later chapters.

Mental Detritus

In civilized humangee society, we generally try to look after our body, our home, our security, and our overall well-being.

We wash to keep the parts of the body-device clean, including teeth, hair, and skin. Some keep their homes tidy, as it enables them to find things and avoid the accumulation of clutter, to maintain good hygiene, and thus ensure a productive environment.

However, there is little attention given to the mind and emotional heart. Few people are aware of what they're allowing to fester in their internal cupboards.

Look after your mind (and UR body)

Where else are you going to live?

Whether we like it or not, believe it or not, we build up mental deposits and clutter over time.

Few people cultivate a daily or weekly habit of cleaning the mind and heart; there's rarely even an annual spring clean. Over time, clutter and debris accumulate. This DOES have consequences, which are rarely properly explained and not well understood.

Largely unintended, this accumulation of mental waste, ideas, perceptions, irritations, phobias, superstitions, hang-ups, unfounded concepts, and self-undermining notions does the humangee a huge disservice.

As a consequence, humangee may compromise their mental health. In other words, we maintain low levels of mental fitness. Most of us would probably fail the humangee "mental fit for purpose" test.

These mental health deficits range from depression to unhappiness to lack of motivation to boredom to underperformance. Some simply drift along, failing to take responsibility for their physical health, seeking pleasures and activities that release them from the challenges of being alone with their thoughts, worries, fears, bad habits, and concerns.

Additionally, poor mental values result in humans that are not attuned with natural laws; consequently, they experience cognitive and physical dissonance (i.e., they get sick, ill, develop chronic ailments, or suffer in some other internal capacity). These generally happen over time. For a large majority, the current generations of humangee are not comfortable operating with the way things are. In short, most of us have difficulty accepting our own reality.

To be clear, the natural state for a humangee, when properly looked after, is joyful, fun, light, productive, and contented. It is in its nature to live this way.

Fixed versus Scalable Capacity and Utilization

Let's say you have a mobile device with an XYZ processing chip and 256 GB of storage space; then you rent 100 GB of cloud storage space. The onboard capacity of your phone is static, as it's designed to be.

Humangee, on the other hand, start with a flexible capacity core chip, a massive adaptive processor and flexible on-device storage, and infinite cloud-based storage and access—all included in the deal.

The opportunity for the humangee custodian is to nurture the device in the early years to cultivate a sense of wonder in their device, to experiment with it and use it for their chosen field of endeavor. In order to do so, they should understand the rules of operation and enable humangee to live and enjoy life and the creation to its full capacity.

However, most current custodians do not fully appreciate this opportunity.

Accessing Humangee's Huge Capacity: Opportunity and Responsibility

Humangee all have the same basic design and capacity utilization opportunity at the level of essence. The job or prospect for the custodian is to make good use of the capacity.

Device and Access to Content

The internet provides myriad resources for everyone: students, journalists, parents, workers, businesspeople, educators, researchers, and so on. These resources are available and accessible to anyone with a device to access the content. Our device is not limited by the content that resides on its fixed drive, irrespective of the size.

The humangee mind is like a mobile device that is able to access the wider available content, insight, intuition, and more. We have been programmed to think of "my mind and my intellect."

It is not that one humangee mind (not brain) is different than another, it's just that they are different devices accessing the collective resource.

Our individual mind and its capacity are simply a device by which we gain access to a much bigger resource. We are not limited by what we perceive that we have direct access to in our own mind or the worldly resources that we can read or listen to.

I suspect that you have questions on this, but bear with me. ☺

Training Fleas and Humangee

Fleas, humangee, and other living organisms are alike in that they can all be trained or conditioned.

Consider an updated version of the classic flea trainer story:

Fleas principally do two things; they ride around on animals and they jump. To train a flea to be a low jumper, you put it in a jar and contain it with the lid. Without the lid, of course, the flea will jump right out of the jar. Apparently, they can jump two hundred times their height!

Once you have your flea or fleas in the jar, you put a lid on the jar. If you watch, the flea will jump-bump, jump-bump, jump-bump, jump-bump. Is it strong willed, or is it stupid, or is it just in its nature? You might leave it for twenty minutes and come back to find it's still going jump-bump, jump-bump, hitting its head on the lid. Come back in an hour, and it may not be hitting the lid quite as hard, but it's still going at it: jump-bump, jump-bump, jump-bump.

At some stage in the next three hours, the flea realizes it is subject to Einstein's definition of insanity: one doing the same thing again and again and expecting a different result. On this realization, the flea changes tack and modifies its jumping pattern. It then jumps a bit lower and less vigorously, managing to stop just before the lid. Flea life is now okay again, and it goes about the normal business of jumping to the new height with full vigor.

Your flea has now been trained.

Take the lid off the jar. Even then the flea will still stick to its new regime. It will not jump higher than the level of the lid. It has forgotten that it could once jump out of the jar.

Humangee are like the flea. Each one has extraordinary capacity at birth, but inadvertent conditioning by themselves and well-meaning others results in humangee not appreciating what they are capable of and designed for.

Your flea can't distinguish between a lid and a self-imposed belief or limitation.

Likewise, humangee generally don't distinguish between real and self-imposed constraints until they get the opportunity to "wake up," to see the bigger picture.

With your humangee manual in hand, you can realize that your humangee may have been "flea trained." Now is the time to untrain or reprogram your device to encourage it to make full use of its capacity. For the self and the joy and good of all.

Humangee Trained Mind

Humangee has been trained against the use of the wider universal mind; thus, our capacity to access it is hindered. Most take for granted the device that they manage. We do not see or appreciate the wonderful device, and so its full capacity is rarely recognized or activated. More importantly, there is a much bigger, but more subtle resource and capability that we can tap into if we choose to. In some cases, our environment or our choices may make it difficult to access.

The use, or non-use, of this capacity applies in all aspects of our lives: survival, family, work, relationships, dealing with challenges, hobbies, sport, leisure, learning, awakening, and more.

This natural adaption response is evident throughout nature. For example, Koi fish often grow in relation to the size of their tank. As small as 7–8 cm in a small tank and as large as 15–20 cm in a larger tank or pond. Nature and its creatures respond and evolve to the constraints applied.

Junk Values

We all understand the concept of junk foods. They have become so commonplace that they are now deemed normal and acceptable. We also know that they affect the humangee physically and mentally, especially when consumed in excess. The same goes for junk values.

The consequences of consuming junk food are obvious in the material world, while the consequences of mental junk are more subtle.

Junk values are everywhere, and most people are not awake to them. Without an understanding of the fundamental laws and guidelines, most people are oblivious to the level of misconception or misunderstanding that we are exposed to. We have grown up with fake news on how to live.

The junk values do for the mind and heart what the junk food does for the body-device. It is not good.

These comprise a whole host of perceptions that are now deemed acceptable:

- That it's okay to harbor grudges and get irritated at ourselves and others.
- That it's okay for the mind to run rampant in whatever way it wants.
- That it's okay to live an unbalanced life.
- That it's okay to treat other people as being fundamentally different from us and wonder why we don't get harmonious outcomes.
- That it's okay to consume more fuel than we need without suffering consequences.
- That it's okay not to take responsibility for self and others.
- That it's okay to harbor a range of negative emotions (e.g., envy, greed, hatred) and not expect a consequence.
- That it's okay to use a mobile phone for four hours a day or more and not expect to be influenced by the content and the habits that develop.
- That it's okay to watch TV until one in the morning and get up for work at seven, and not expect this to have a detrimental impact.

Junk values lead to junk outcomes.

What to do with the pollutants in the mind and heart?

The good news is, humangee do have power to affect the accumulation of the detritus in the mind and heart. But it helps to understand what we are dealing with.

Many humangee, of all ages, are now exposed to nonstop global interaction around the clock.

There is little to no scope for "downtime" due to the current prevailing culture and technology.

It's already well-proven that significant harm is done by excessive screen time and dependence on online social interaction.

Just like smoking affects physical health, the damage and destruction on mental health is already well documented and will become clear over time.

Humangee have a tendency to develop patterns that determine behaviors, interactions, activities, and focus, which in turn inform our habits, routines, and frame of mind. These practices have a strong influence on whether we are able to enjoy the journey. In short, these mental routines determine our lives. Our experience of this life is controlled by the software in our head.

The good news is that we can begin to observe these patterns. This is firmly within our control. We need to understand the effects and consequences and then take action as appropriate.

The bad news is, the degradation will continue to progress until the core issues are addressed. Understanding or observing these pollutants without taking action is fruitless.

Knowledge without Action Is Fruitless

This humangee tendency to know what to do yet not do it is another effect of delusion, a consequence of not taking full responsibility for ourselves. It is vital to appreciate that understanding these concepts is useful. However, understanding without action is the "wooden spoon." The *wooden spoon* is the hypothetical prize for the person or team finishing in last place in a competition.

Thus, participants in a competition are reminded to keep their eye on the prize. We must know why we are doing what we

are doing. This positive pressure can bring clarity about the consequences of not doing what needs to be done.

The wooden spoon

Humangee Are Like a Cell

A diseased cell will harm all of those around it and stimulate the spread of disease unless it comes up against resistance. Likewise, a healthy cell supports and nourishes those around it to keep the whole organism strong.

As a humangee, we have the choice to be a healthy cell and to have a positive as opposed to negative impact on all around us.

Care in Communications: Understanding the Impact on Unawakened Humangee

Language, awakeness, and intent are subtly but vitally important to the impressionable humangee at every age.

Clear, specific, attentive words and language can bring hugely positive effects. Harsh, critical, and abusive words and language can cause devastatingly negative effects. And these negative imprints can remain with a humangee for a long time, often forever.

To use the old cliché, "a sentence is a sentence."

A throwaway comment can be metaphorically like a prison sentence.

Words are causal, and different people use them habitually in different ways. They are often used on automatic pilot, with little real thought. In addition, words and their effects form part of our habitual thinking and ultimately become second nature; they become our thought processes. This is true whether the words are positive or negative. We can observe this in ourselves and others.

It is vital that you are awake and attuned, particularly when giving words to another humangee. When talking with others, particularly in difficult situations, people will ultimately not remember what was said—they will remember how you made them feel.

Try to be as conscious and attentive as possible when listening and speaking. A useful practice to support you in this effort is to consciously listen to the sound of your own voice and notice the effect. It should be a positive exercise, as you need to be in the present to do it, which is not always easy.

Do not speak untruths, speak the truth kindly.

Buddha recommended: If you propose to speak, always ask yourself, is it true, is it necessary, is it kind?

It helps to pause before we speak, to ensure we are awake.

The Field

A number of scriptures contain an analogy: the humangee mind is like a field. Imagine a field scattered with trash: tin cans, blue bags, old bricks, broken down cars, shopping carts. There might even be a fenceless part where the fly-tippers[4] have got in and dumped a bit of old furniture and rubble. Remember the mental detritus we spoke of earlier?

So we work to rid the mind of obvious misconceptions. We learn about paying attention and the enormous difference it makes. We should maintain the principle of pausing and bring the mind to stillness (even if only for a second) whenever we can.

Our job is to clean the field of our mind

4 A fly-tipper is someone who dumps their trash in an unauthorized place.

Chapter 8
Maintenance, Error Signals, Fuel, Power

This may be a contentious subject. Our paradigms as a civilized society and our development over the last hundred years have become accepting of humangee's propensity to do things with the body, mind, and heart that are counter to what nature intended.

For example, many humangee readily engage in smoking or vaping, ingesting hot fumes derived from the burning of dried leaves known to contain carcinogens and having addictive capabilities.

This is only one of the many self-sabotaging habits humangee undertake. These risks are enabled by lack of awakeness—individually and collectively. Most are created by new product and service offerings driven largely by commercial organizations with almost solely financial objectives. Compounding the effects, other industries have piggy-backed to benefit also, like legal, insurance, finance, and others. Many of us work within these companies or know someone who does, benefiting financially from these products and services. We are part of the system.

Our medical system has historically focused on treating disease and ailments rather than promoting and facilitating health.

The deficiencies in these areas are well chronicled—it's the paradigms that got us here that should be properly examined. We need to realize as a society that in terms of living to our potential, the current paradigms won't get us to where we want to go.

To use another old cliché, if you do what you always did, you'll get what you always got. If we want a different outcome, then we need to face reality across a number of areas.

Mind and Body Are One and the Same System

Most people would say it's ridiculous to suggest that the respiratory system does not affect the digestive system or that the nerve system doesn't affect the musculoskeletal system. They appreciate that they are both part of the whole.

But what about the mind and body? The same applies to the mind. If you ask humangee about the link between the mind and body, they are not sure about the connection or they assume it is tenuous. The reality is that the body and mind are as interdependent as any other biological systems. Because the device is one whole system. Not two.

So, what does this mean for humangee? The good news is that humangee in its natural form is very resilient and can therefore put up with quite a lot of variation and some imbalance. But if it is taken far out of balance, in terms of fuels, toxins, physical or mental demands, or chronic lack of sleep, the body-device, the mind, and the heart suffer consequences.

With regard to the body aspects, it is designed to be used for walking, working of all types, cleaning, running, helping, child-raising, building, sitting, hunting, cooking, playing, and other physical activities.

In light of these truths, we should be conscious of how we fuel and maintain our device—physically and mentally.

We should also be aware of the natural laws that apply. **And be absolutely clear that our mind and body are inextricably linked and interdependent.**

Humangee Fuel and Power

Humangee consume fuel, which is then converted to energy or in some cases put into storage as fat. The fuel we put into humangee is absolutely central to its development.

Humangee has been evolving steadily on the planet over many years. It has traditionally consumed an increasing range of foods. Some would suggest that this has contributed over the last few thousand years to the humangee brain component evolving more quickly.

However, over the last hundred years, farming, lifestyle, and other changes have delivered more food and food types at increasingly cost-effective rates. However, not all foodstuffs are equal.

In particular, highly processed foods are having an increasingly detrimental impact on the humangee race.

With regard to the carnivore-herbivore debate, our consumption of other animals creates a growing problem. It's up to each of us to educate ourselves around this aspect and take conscious action to address it.

Over the last sixty years, the use of sugar in its various derivations has grown hugely. It is singularly one of the most detrimental intoxicants willingly ingested to overload humangee instruments. Like a tsunami, it is spreading across the world and resulting in a host of human appliance error signals, performance reduction, and system breakdowns.

A typical example is that of type 2 diabetes, predominately driven by consumption of excessive sugar and refined foods, reduced physical activity, and associated interactions, resulting in wider system malfunction.

Body Mass Index (BMI)

The BMI across the world has risen steadily over the last fifty years as consumer consumption patterns have transformed globally. School playground activity levels have dropped, and obesity is on the rise at increasingly younger ages.

Simple rules to fuel your humangee:

1. Make time to prepare food/meals
2. Make time to eat in a mindful way
3. Eat slowly, taste your food
4. It is not necessary to eat until you are full
5. Consume a wide variety of foods
6. Love yourself enough to find out what you could and should eat
7. Drink plenty of clean water
8. Minimize refined sugars
9. Prioritize fresh fruits, vegetables, nuts, pulses, and natural foods

Take Care of Your Spine

Your spine, your backbone, is the core chain that runs from the top-rear of your head all the way down your body. It is the trunk that serves and supports muscles, nerves, and more. Look after it with use and gentle regular exercise and it will look after you. Yoga and Pilates practices are good.

Breathing

We take breathing for granted. It is the foundation for a good supply of oxygen into our body-system, and a cornerstone to good physical and mental health.

Rarely do we pause to check whether we are using our lungs and diaphragm fully. When breathing is out of balance, the diaphragm, abdomen, and pelvis tend to be out of equilibrium also. Additionally, poor breathing is almost always combined with physical stiffness and poor posture: a curved spine, rigid pelvis, and tense shoulders disturb the balance of the body. They restrict blood flow and chest capacity and are often associated with stress and anxiety, collectively causing shallow breathing, which contributes to physical and mental disease.

Hence observing your breathing and posture regularly is a useful part of your pauses and practice.

Much of the rest of the chapter deals with the subtle, mental software aspects. Because this affects both hardware and software, self-help, support, and maintenance recommendations are offered below.

Error Signals

Sometimes humor is the best teacher. When "Human Error Signals" was considered, the first thing that came to mind was the classic pantomime in which the villain is on the stage with the lead character, and the crowd shouts, **"He's behind you."**

The hapless heroine looks behind and around her, again and again, but continually misses the "up-to-no-good" bad guy.

Humangee and their error signals are a bit like that. They appear all around us, but we are doing other things. We're too busy to notice. We think that lesser or mundane issues are more important. We either don't see them or we just choose to ignore them.

Firstly, most humangee do not have a true baseline on what a natural state should be. That is, we are not totally clear on what a completely healthy and naturally operating humangee experience is. Hence, we are missing the vital reference point against which to measure.

Most reading this will by now have been intoxicated with activities, mental noise, sugar-laden food, and various other distractions to the extent they will have forgotten what true normal feels like.

Ask any professional athlete. Ask any truly awakened practitioner. What is a good baseline in their field? And while we may not necessarily aspire to these levels, we can make significant progress in moving toward the health of body and mind.

As we've said: body and mind are linked. Device and software are both needed for humangee to operate and flourish. If you do something good for the body, you do something good for the mind by default. And vice versa. That's just how it works; it's in the rules.

So, what kind of error signals should we be looking out for? Error signals from a car or a computer arise when something is not working properly. Because that's what we expect—that things behave as they are designed to.

The reality is that humans are so far removed from what natural looks and feels like that we don't treat things that should be error signals as signals; dysfunctions have simply become a new norm.

So, things like irritation, frustration, anger, discontentment, lethargy, depression, guilt, chronic exhaustion, etc. These are signals that there is some form of discord.

As the custodian, you can observe these in your device and identify which to address.

One device

All aspects work in harmony

Use-It-or-Lose-It Function

The humangee is a biped; it moves in its natural form on two legs. It is an evolved physical device that benefits from regular movement, and that's what its current iteration is designed for.

Increasingly, though, humangee sits on the section where the body folds easily in the forward direction—the seat or bum. There are other key fold joints in the main limbs with some of the branches displaying complex capability. These include arms, elbows, hands, and fingers with joints and pads that have the ability to touch and sense with a high degree of dexterity. There are capacities used by different custodians to varying degrees.

One of the beautiful efficiencies of this embodiment is the "use-it-or-lose-it" function.

In complex terms, this is an autonomous self-managed device optimization mechanism that internally focuses resources and neural specific development into the functional areas where the custodian has decided they want them to go.

So, a humangee deciding to be a weight-lifter will develop muscles in the designated and trained areas. Hence the development over time will be significantly different to the one choosing to be a pianist, tennis star, or chess player. In simple terms, if you don't use a muscle, you lose it, or it atrophies over time. This is another example of the law of entropy at work!

This fantastic attribute enables humangee to use its range of faculties to become proficient in a hugely diverse range of ways.

This principle applies to the physical, mental, emotional, and other areas.

Specifically, one has the opportunity to exercise the positive, affirmative, happiness, laughing, loving, helping,

serving, problem-solving muscles. Or one could choose the gossiping, back-biting, misery-focused, irritated, belittling mental muscles.

The choice is entirely up to each humangee custodian. Each approach delivers its own particular result. **You choose the mental muscles you use or lose.**

Remember, your humangee is naturally like a puppy: It loves the outdoors. It likes to run and play, to jump and wrestle. It enjoys a regular set of stretches. It lives to give love and attention to others; it rests between activities. The natural laughing, loving, happy, caring muscles will engage and develop if allowed and encouraged.

Consider that happiness, laughter, contentment, freedom, peace, and love are muscles. Are you using or losing?

❚❚

Device Idle Time

One of the other subtle changes in recent years is the attention span of an average humangee. Apparently, it is now less than twenty seconds. ("What is?" I hear you ask.) Hence why many soap operas and films feature short segments to keep the audience engaged.

So, if you use a laptop or mobile device, you will know that, depending on what setting you've chosen, the wallpaper or screensaver will effectively take over the screen once the idle time has elapsed.

Humangee have a similar "Revert to dream state" mode that takes over many times a day. But most don't realize that their device is in sleep mode and they can continue to dream in this mode, either in the past or future (i.e., their mind is not fully focused on the task at hand or present with the current activity).

As the custodian, you can direct your device to develop a habit of checking in.

- Pause
- Ask, *Am I dreaming?*
- Ask, *Am I present?*
- Inquire, *Am I giving undiluted attention to what I am doing?*
- What senses are in use?
- Or is the device idle, just drifting along?
- What's my energy state?

The Mobile Phone Malware Debacle

Earlier versions of the humangee device had the option to switch off and reboot regularly. The advent of the mobile phone, combined with the Ego Virus, has essentially created a perfect storm.

The humangee device can't go into silent mode for refresh; it is bombarded by me-and-my and how-I-feel programs, which

maintain addictive mind activity. It is a vicious circle that we can now clearly see leading to a SAD (System Affecting Disorder) error.

The observed effect of this error over the last few years is the atrophy of the mental balance of the humangee, with a wide range of consequent effects. For our species of humangee, these go by a range of medical and non-medical names and effects. The poor humangee is in a permanent dream state, asleep to nature and their true being in a depressed state with external fixation, a sense of loss of control, and reduction in their perception of self-worth.

This then has knock-on effects in other parts of the body, mind, and heart.

Our ability to communicate directly, face to face, appears to be declining. We need to be aware of the dependencies or attachments that we are developing to our phones, and we must be awake to the consequences.

Reboot, Reset, Recalibrate

Microsoft Windows users (and users of other operating systems too) may be aware of such scenarios when the device is not performing as it should. Sometimes you can't open a folder or the functionality has slowed down. In some cases the screen just locks and won't work at all. The first and simplest solution is to reboot. That is, turn it off and on again—for you nerds, power cycle. You'll be happy to hear that the humangee device has a similar reboot option.

Sometimes things build up, we get tired or irritable, or we're too close to a job, project, or challenge. Maybe we have had an emotional or difficult conversation with a friend, partner, or loved one. These are all cases in which a reset is helpful and should allow the device to refresh and work cleanly, clearly, and efficiently.

The key is to build a series of practices that work for your device. You're looking for practices that allow the body-mind to be still, relaxed, detached, present, and properly awake. If you can learn to do this quickly and regularly, and then act from the new position of clarity and love, you will have developed a master skill.

Combining this with sleep is helpful too.

You are literally rebooting your device.

"Why didn't someone tell me?" you ask. Well, now you know. ☺

The humangee device experiences a whole spectrum of system efficiency drops, caused by a wide range of factors, most of which are within our control. Our habits, diet, interactions, unmanaged thought suggestions, willingness to accept other people's opinions of us—all of these affect our system operation. The reboot practices will benefit all of these areas.

"So, all I need to do is fall still, be present, stay relaxed, and observe my breathing and each of my senses?"

Yep. That's it. And the more you practice it, the easier and more useful it becomes.

Diagnostic Tools for the Device

What tools do we have to understand the state of the control software, applications, and storage media?

Consider a farcical situation.

The farce is that there is little appreciation or agreement on the nature of the components that are to be diagnosed. And, thus, there is an unclear model of the subcomponents to analyze. Hence any diagnosis is partial, incomplete, misinformed, and misleading.

So, the requirement is to agree and validate a baseline set of components for which we have a basic understanding of how they operate and interact.

See the following diagram as an example, to help clarify.

From there we can establish what good looks like for each component and the overall model.

When we know that, we can then observe the variances, understand them, and establish ways by which we can measure that variance.

We are then in a position to diagnose and recommend remedies and actions.

The next challenge is implementation.

Humangee have a poor track record for self-fixing. That is, people often know what to do, but for various reasons, they don't or can't follow through.

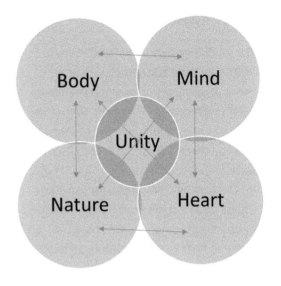

Recommendations

Self-responsibility: Reflect on each of your component parts—body, mind, heart and nature—and take a view on variance (what's not right) on the position from the perfect natural state.

This sounds difficult, but it doesn't have to be. Use rebooting to reset: pause, practice mindfulness, get still, and be present or truly awake.

We'll discuss these recommendations in more detail in section 2.

> *In minds crammed with thoughts, organs clogged with toxins, and bodies stiffened with neglect, there is just no space for anything else.*
>
> —Alison Rose Levy, health journalist and coach

This concludes the direct comparison with a mobile or computing device. The next section looks in more detail at the functional aspects of the components in everyday living and how they operate together, if allowed to.

Section 2

In-life Management

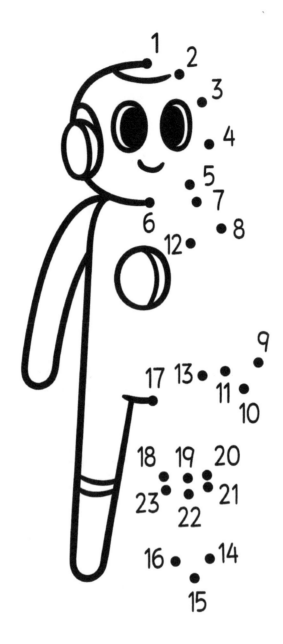

Connect the Dots

Are you appreciating the whole you or just a part? Maybe you understand the physical, external aspects of your being but not the subtle. Something is missing but you are not sure what.

You are in fact already whole but are just not awake to the other part. Maybe when you are present, you might experience it, appreciate it, get to live as a complete humangee. Will you join the dots, or will you remain oblivious to the other part forever?

Using This Manual

This section has been structured to follow a logical sequence, building on earlier parts and principles. There are some concepts that have been separated out for further clarification.

Throughout the manual, you may see repetition, overlapping of concepts, and repeated recommendations. This is due to the fact that once the core understanding and framework is established, things start to fall into place, and the whole set of concepts, which we already know intuitively, should start to coalesce like a jigsaw puzzle or a connect the dots activity.

Models and Concepts

Readers may not necessarily agree with all the "models" put forward, as some may require further explanation, clarifications, and distinctions.

The theme and basis on which they are built is sound; has been tested over years, by philosophers, inquirers, and other thought leaders; and is a useful starting point for personal assessment and further self-inquiry.

This model simplifies life experience and operation of the software at mind level into two key worlds or aspects:

Transient and Permanent

Transient describes the external world, which is constantly changing, with some parts moving faster than others. Transient comprises the physical aspects of our world: science, senses, and sense-objects. It is the day-to-day life that we experience in our mind and thoughts.

Permanent or *Eternal* describes that which is essentially unchanging and comprises key aspects of the internal software environment.

It includes the subtle aspects of unity and nature, and deals with natural, internal laws.

The various mental exercises found within this section aim to help the user gain direct experience, like the silence behind the sounds that we hear and the stillness behind the activities that we are engaged in. It is only experienced in the present, in a state of being.

The term *truth* reflects that which is permanent.

We will start with five distinctions, or aspects, that will form a framework for what follows.

1. Body

2. Heart

3. Mind

4. Nature

5. Awareness

Awareness

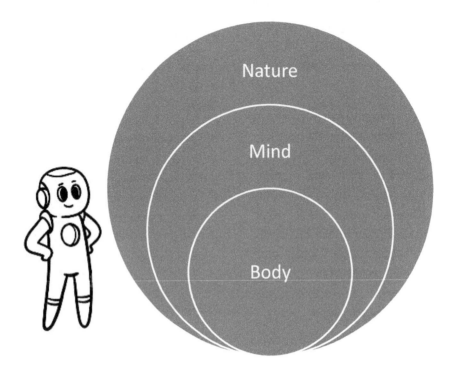

These will be described in more detail in the following chapters.

So happy jig-sawing. ☺

Chapter 9

The Present Moment

Current Reality for Most Ordinary Humangee

Humans are the only animal concerned with time, and consequently the only one for which it causes a problem. Where the past and future dominate, they do not add to one's happiness. They result in a life where opportunities are never fully experienced, exploited, enjoyed, or lived.

So, if humangee can't break free from this bondage, their life will be far short of what it could have been.

It is also one of the positive, creative, wondrous aspects of the humangee, which allows us to imagine and pre-envision, as well as retain and utilize information.

When past and future dominate your thoughts, life just flies by: you only taste a small percentage of that cup of coffee, or you miss half of the car journey, or you space out for half of that conversation. If you don't wake your humangee up, it is like a bus trip where every so often one of you asks, "How did we get here? Is this where I wanted to be?" If you are lucky, you may get regular stops in your teens, twenties, thirties, forties, fifties, through to the final bus stop, where you might acknowledge that you could have enjoyed so much more joy, service, and happiness in your life.

The Present Moment and Why It's so Important

The present moment is where all your senses are awake and your attention is focused on what is in front of you right now. It can be active or passive.

Your mind is clear and you are focused on the task at hand. It could be washing the dishes, tidying around the house, talking to a friend, or engaging with work. You are 100% present.

Remember in chapter 6, we outlined the different states of attention. In the present moment, one is centered. In this state, things are done with precision and joy, to the best of one's ability. You are awake and alive and able to respond appropriately to what arises. There is a level of focus but also detachment, where challenges can seem easier to handle.

The diagram below shows that it is one of the eternal laws and fundamental aspects that apply in determining how our software is operating.

Ego

Discursive mind

True reason

Heart

Energy states

Aware, Dull, Fervent

Eternal Laws

Love, Responsibility, Unity, Wisdom
Present Moment,

Cause & Effect, Essence,

Still Mind   Active Mind

Allow the mind to fall still

For a fuller explanation there are numerous books and resources, including *The Power of Now* by Eckhart Tolle and *Awareness* by Anthony de Mello.

Not Living in the Present

The present moment is like a point in geometry. It has no measure of time. For humangee, there is a line in front and a line behind that tend to get all the focus. Future imaginations and memories of the past can be positive or negative. Both disappear in the now. However, if humangee is not connected to the present moment, past and future govern through emotions like fear, hope, dread, irritation, disappointment, excitement, dreaming, and sentimentality. Past and future cannot ever offer full satisfaction.

What Causes Us to Leave the Present Moment?

- **Addictive thinking**. We have allowed ourselves, in most cases, to equate thinking with efficiency. We fill the space with thoughts, not allowing room for the mind to come to rest. Some even feel guilty when they are not actively thinking. **It's useful to appreciate (or consider) that this is a real problem.**

- **Unresolved issues and events. We hold on to** these unnecessarily; this could be anything from repairs at home, unfinished work, old irritations, and maybe even to-do lists extended beyond what is reasonable to do within the next year.

- **Idleness.** There are times when we are not fully engaged with what's in front of us. We are drifting because, for whatever reason, we do not see the task at hand as worthy of focused attention.

- **Desire and aversion.** Unawake humangee are always seeking something: either moving toward something (desire) or away from something (aversion). We are always going somewhere and never being here. We live for the weekend, for the summer, for Christmas break. Our happiness becomes conditional on something in the future.

If we are not living fully in the present when things are happening, we don't get full satisfaction. And since we don't get full satisfaction, we either desire to repeat things over and over again or seek new things to undertake (i.e., we continue the search for something that will yield full satisfaction).

- **Running commentaries in the mind.** As we discussed in chapter 6, the discursive mind enables the production of a constant flow of ideas and thoughts. In this case, they are often judgmental in nature and frequently based on small, rigid views or ideas. It is useful to be awake to these and ask, *Who do they serve?*

What Is the Effect of Living a Life in the Past and Future?

- **Not present for everyday living.** To an extent, we become absent from our own lives. We are not fully there to enjoy all the subtleties that occur every day. Our minds clutter with stuff, and we short-change our partner, our friends, our children, or our work or business. The net effect is we don't do things properly, resulting in reactiveness rather than responsiveness. We develop predictable patterns and prejudices, and stagnate, leaving little room for new approaches and possibilities.

Fear becomes part of our life. So instead of dealing with what is happening, we try to deal with what might happen. Because we are not present, we do not handle

life well. It's like our sense of acuity has moved down a notch. We are slower to see things, like cars in our peripheral vision, like the nuances of the communications of those around us. We tend to be surprised by the things happening in our life.

A subtle world of anxiety, worry, stress, nervousness, unease, phobia, and dread results—all caused by not being in the present. If these are left unchecked, they will accumulate over time.

One might argue they're making contingency plans and preparing for future scenarios. Common sense should apply in that case. It is not possible to truly deal with ten or twenty potential outcomes. But we can deal with the present very effectively, as there is only one thing happening.

- **Always striving, never arriving.** We are always trying to be something else or get somewhere different or do something other than what's here in the now. So, for most of us, life becomes a means to an end. We continually believe that success or happiness is just around the corner.

Always striving, never arriving

In this way, you spend your life thinking things will be better when … I have got my school exams finished, then it'll be great if I can get into university.

It'll be fantastic when … I graduate.

Things will fall into place when … I get my first job and start earning some money.

Life will really start when … I meet someone that I really connect with. And on and on. Often the happiness is postponed now, and we are continually chasing something new.

Bank and celebrate your achievements, no matter how small. You can just be and enjoy where you have arrived to, right now. It really is possible!

Avoid the obsessive need to attain, and be able to say, "I have made it. I have arrived." When you postpone truly living, the quality of your actions is reduced because it is focused on future rather than carrying out the action now. Because the end is the reward, it takes the joy out of doing. In this mode, becoming is substituted for being.

A Word about Hope

While some may say that hope keeps us going, we need to be vigilant, or it denies the joy of now. Stress comes from being here and wishing we were there, when we are dissatisfied with the now. This view then continues to reinforce humangee away from being present.

- **We give the future and past a life.** By not living in the present, we dig up old stuff unnecessarily. It's like pulling up an old DVD, MP3, or YouTube clip and playing it again and again. We're dreaming our unfounded deluding into the future.

The Experience of Just Being

What is life like when someone lives in the present?

- The mind becomes still, awake, and reflective. It is NOT active, planning, distorting, and rehearsing. The mind reveals what it knows. Pure intelligence, knowledge arising in the moment, enables dealing with the situation perfectly. We know what to do and we do it to the best of our ability.

- There is no internal dialogue, no doubt, no hesitation. There is responding in place of reacting to life as it arises before us. It gives a simple and tremendous freedom.

Some people use exhilarating pursuits like bungee jumping or moving well outside their comfort zone to bring them into the present. That is not necessary. We simply make the decision, fall still, or give our focused attention to the task at hand and to our senses and we are there (we can have free exhilaration, on demand, every day).

- In the present, we encounter events—not problems—and enjoy the distinction. When we do this, there are no more problems. Just events. No worries, no anxiety, no fear.

One learns to be detached. We look at our problems in the same way that we might look at someone else's; with a level of clinical clarity. Hence, in the now, we deal with situations or events that need to be dealt with. Or in many cases they just need to be let go.

We see that which is in front of us as our teacher.

We get a present every day.

A present of the present

If on completing this section or book you can take away one thing, this would be it. Realise that your ability to be consistently in the present moment can change your life. It is beyond the best birthday gift you could ever receive.

- The heart opens and we are naturally happier, since we experience peace and joy—right now.

Life in the now is being, not becoming. The heart is free of burdens, and we don't carry that pesky past and future around with us. The humangee becomes light and bright. We see beauty in everything, the essence in all, and the unity in all. All religions have their description for this place, and it's good.

When truly in the now, you can keep the company of limitless bliss and give it whatever name you choose.

In the now, there is an experience of presence and joy that is not dependent on any external thing. So, it doesn't matter what your station in life, whether prince, pauper, or anything in between. In this regard we are all equal. And sometimes it can be easier for those who have experienced more hardships to hear the wake-up call.

- In the present, we see that which is in front of us as our teacher. We see the essence in people and things around us.

Bringing the Mind into the Present Moment

So, how can we bring the mind into the present moment?

Practice True Acceptance

We embrace the present moment, warts and all. This is Acceptance with a capital A. It means that we embrace all of life. Yes, all of it. We welcome all of it, the good and the bad.

This is a vital concept. To the extent that we cannot accept our life as it is, we will experience pain. It's quite simple.

Resistance to the present moment is pain. That pain pushes one to the past or the future. It's not the present that is painful, but one's resistance to it.

So, the key is not to retreat to past or future but to meet your life in the present and experience it. And if there is something to be addressed, then address it right here and now.

Connect with the Senses

When you connect with the senses, you are in the present moment. You can only see, hear, taste, and smell what is occurring now. You can't taste a future burger or a past apple. So, when you are in the rain, experience the soft wetting effect. There is no need to add misery or irritation. You have the opportunity to experience dampness, which is lovely if you are accepting of it.

The present moment offers only contentment. If we add anything to it, it becomes less, and in some cases, tends toward misery.

This is exactly the same as mindfulness, where we are fully present and engaged with the senses.

The opportunity is to be mindful with the everyday events of life—walking, eating, shaving, working, studying, putting one's clothes on. In a mindful state, all the little movements become special.

The focus is on the action now, and not on the outcome or results. If the action is done with attention in the present, it will be completed with precision and joy and will deliver an appropriate output at its very best.

Be alert to when the mind is focused purely on the results and not the action, as it will result in a reduction in the quality, efficiency, and joy.

Connect with the Permanent

Remember that the *transient* is the temporal world of day-to-day life, where things come and go, time passes. It is the world of the body, where during a lifetime, cars change, buildings go up and down, roads are added, civilization is expanded in urban areas, and cellular masts are changed. This external, earthly life is full of change. In fact, change is the only constant aspect to it.

The *permanent* or eternal aspects of existence are those that do not change. This is the silence upon which all sounds are allowed to resonate; it is the stillness that underpins all activity. None of these underlying aspects is broken or disturbed by the activity. Things aren't very complicated in stillness, they just *are*.

Learn to discriminate, to see or know the difference between permanent and transient.

So, if your attention is only given to the transient, then the mind drifts into the future and past.

If it acknowledges the eternal and permanent, and remains in the present, it is thus able to enjoy the transient. (As Hanna Montana would say, you get the best of both worlds).

If we connect with what is eternal and always present, we will be unmoved by the transient and able to rest in the activities of life.

Finding the stillness, we find the present.

Conclusions:

Learn to experience love and life now, not the results of life.

Stop waiting for something to happen for life to be better.

Take your rest now, take your freedom now.

Take your joy now, take your peace now.

Live the rest of your life—in the now.

Chapter 10
Happiness Is the Natural State

Happiness is a prevailing state of well-being, joy, and contentment.

In its true sense, it is not transient but permanent and pervades the being on an ongoing basis. It is the natural state of being for humangee.

It has been well established through research and observation that most actions have happiness as their root motive, but it is not always the resulting outcome.

Many humangee do not get to experience permanent happiness as a natural state, as their level of contentment moves up and down like a wave.

A stream of ups and downs, and in some cases not many ups.

Pleasure, for the purposes of this book, is a pursuit of happiness. As opposed to the simple natural pleasures, it is often sought through getting away from the challenges and perceived difficulties of day-to-day life. It could be through holidays, food, television, addiction to phone, socializing, shopping, buying or having nice things, or achievement of or attachment to a desired outcome. Hence it relates more to the gaining and trying of external things that bring a sense of satisfaction. It's a form of escapism. Like a drug, most of these types of pleasure are temporal and are the fulfill-ment of wants and desires, which by their nature yield only temporary satisfaction, only to be replaced by the same or other similar desire tomorrow.

They have an insatiable nature, and thus are unable to be fully satisfied.

Desire is a craving, longing, or yearning. A strong feeling that you want something that impels you to the attainment or possession of that which is potentially within reach, (e.g., a desire for success). Desires, when channeled properly, can be good, but if not understood and channeled improperly can be harmful.

Misery is a state of discontentment or unhappiness. It can take numerous forms such as helplessness, frustration, sadness, fearfulness, and more. It is an unnatural state for humangee.

Whether we appreciate it or not, it is achieved through choice. This is observable when a level of awareness is achieved. Hence, to someone who is properly awake, choosing misery is a self-inflicted shot to the foot. Misery is generally only experi-enced in the unawake, non-present state.

So, if happiness is the natural state and misery is unnatural, and in most cases is a choice, then happiness is simply what remains in the absence of misery.

Misery is a choice

Where does misery come from?

Misery comes from *mistaken understanding*.

These misunderstandings are often well embedded.

They come as a result of misconceptions that most humangee have distinguishing between true and untrue concepts. The untrue concepts are generally the mindset, paradigm, and delusions that many of us hold today.

Hence there is a need to investigate, to discover what these misunderstandings may be and to establish that there is a viable alternative approach.

The following are some examples:

Natural Values	Misconceptions
Happiness	Pleasure
Knowledge	Information
Fullness of Life	Incessant Activity
Service	Servitude
Generosity (no strings attached)	Give to get
Beauty	Beautiful object
Love	Love for someone or something
Wealth	Money
Truth	True for me
Being true to oneself	Living in the opinions of others
Efficiency	Expediency
Duties before rights	Rights before duties
Work as an expression of happiness	Work as a means to happiness or of survival
Needs	Wants

Being – What am I? (What have I become – progress internally as a humangee?)	Becoming – Status (How am I perceived by the outside world?)
Self-responsibility	Entitlement
?	?

When the natural value is properly understood and lived, true happiness is experienced.

The subtle distinction between each of the concepts on the left and its counterpart on the right could no doubt use more explanation.

Let's take fullness of life as an example. This is an aspiration to maximize our happiness and productivity. However, we often mistake this for busyness, believing that constant focus on outcomes and activity will deliver what we want. Even if we achieve the intermediate goal through busyness, the fullness of life aspiration will not be fully delivered.

Similar distinctions can be made for each pair in the table.

Each humangee has the hand that they have been dealt in life, including the environment, their peers, their initial and subsequent conditioning, and also the misconceptions that they currently hold. All of this then has an impact on how they seek happiness or fulfillment.

Again, happiness is the natural state of being for the essence of a humangee; we are simply striving to realign and reconnect with our true nature.

However, the misinformed and inadvertent choice or practice for many humangee is misery. Many readers may disagree or challenge this, but I invite you to test it through direct experience and observation.

Refine your ability to be present and aligned with the natural value over time, and happiness will be the net result.

Enabling Happiness by Distinguishing Differences in Views of Time and Qualities

Time

A discussion of time must start by appreciating the following:

1. **Passing time**, which is what most people experience each day, is never still. Think of a busy day, the passing of the week, month, and year.

2. **Eternal present**, where there is no mental movement or desires, only simple existence "in the present" as each day or week progresses.

Happiness arises from within and operates in the present moment/eternal present.

So, being content in the present allows one to see that happiness is always available and is here now.

Qualities and Virtues

With regard to qualities and happiness, we will use a model derived from Plato's teaching for key principles.

This model guides or indicates how key choices determine direction and happiness.

There are two types of goods:

- **Divine goods:** wisdom, temperance, courage, and justice
- **Human goods:** health, beauty, strength, and wealth

In terms of precedence and priority, the human goods are secondary to the divine goods.

Happiness dominates when the divine goods are applied in the present.

- **Wisdom:** The knowledge that allows life to be lived truly and happily.
- **Temperance:** Self-control and self-restraint.
- **Courage:** Doing that which should be done; not doing that which should not be done.
- **Justice:** The situation where wisdom governs.

While the other human qualities or goods listed above can be useful and beneficial, they yield less happiness than divine goods.

Is happiness just the habit of experiencing truly awake thoughts in the present?

Happiness: Thoughts to Ponder, Actions to Take

System maintenance recommendations to assist the humangee to align with its natural happiness:

- Behave and live in a way that ALL may be happy.

- Practice serving others: we find our happiness in the happiness of others.

- Make no efforts to become happy. Just be happy—effortlessly.

- Appreciate and enjoy the happiness of deep sleep.

- Happiness is being in tune with one's own nature.

- We create misery generally by holding on to something—there is a need to let go.

- When you observe an irritation or annoyance, allow it a maximum of three seconds—then let it go. Exercise your choice.

- Stop multiple times each day … and just be happy now.

- Stop choosing to be miserable.

- When feeling miserable, ask: "Can I change the way I feel about this?" (Then obey the answer that the mind gives.)

- Make a decision not to sell or give away your happiness (not for anyone or anything—ever).

- Attention and happiness go hand in hand.

- Misery comes from forgetting who and what we are, and is an effect of identifying with our ego, in effect covering our true essence.

- Find the permanent happiness inside rather than the transient one outside.

- When you are fully in the present, you will be awake to the opportunities not to choose the misery.

- It may be useful to remember that desired pleasure does not give true satisfaction.

- The feeling of the incredible marvel of being a human being (not a human becoming).

Chapter 11
Humangee and the Emotional Heart

The Heart and Why It Is Vital

A bit like the CPU (central processing unit) in a computing device, the heart is one of the most important and central parts of humangee—from a mental alignment, congruence, and emotional perspective.

The Bhagavad Gita states that the fools follow the one on the left (physical heart) and the wise follow the one on the right (emotional and spiritual center). This concept is echoed in other philosophies.

So, we have the same word for two things. The English language is less detailed in the lexicon for this inner instrument; there are specific terms for it in Sanskrit and other languages.

The word "heart" in this context is not the physical organ contained in the chest that circulates blood around the body. We perceive that the mind resides in the head, but some philosophies view the subtle mind as residing in the region of the heart. This heart is the source of love, empathy, compassion, and other positive emotions. This heart is closer to the essence of humangee than the mind is. The thinking mind cannot go to the same places the heart can go, as it does not understand it.

The heart is an instrument and also has states.

In its natural state, it is still, perfect, and complete. Like still, clear water, there is no agitation. It simply serves to reflect the soul or essence of humangee.

But like the other instruments, its pure state and its real or live state often differ. It is a core component in our mind model (operating system overview) diagram.

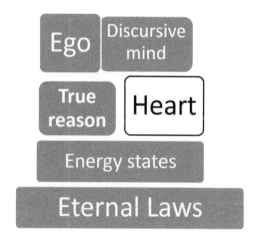

It is described as the seat of emotions for the being. It is not a storehouse for feelings but is the medium to express love.

It is the source of power for the whole being.

- A pure heart is fluid. Nothing leaves a mark. Neither an insult nor a compliment will stick. There is love without attachment.
- In an impure heart the events of life leave their marks, and these become ingrained, often to form various dysfunctional mental habits.

These typically have physical or mental manifestations.

Hence, in most hearts we experience unnecessary emotions. The truth is we do not need to carry them; they serve no purpose other than to burden us.

A Humangee on a Mission

There was an old humangee walking slowly through town, carrying a heavy bag. One day a wise humangee who knew him passed by and asked what he was carrying in the bag. The old man said they were the things he wanted to hold on to. After further discussion, the wise old humangee asked if he could see into the bag.

When his friend opened it, the wise humangee saw it was full of rubbish. He asked, "Why don't you put it down?"

The old humangee replied, "But it's all I have."

We often become attached to long-held emotions and thoughts and don't necessarily recognize them as being useless, burdensome rubbish that we can easily discard if we choose to.

Functioning of the Heart

The heart appears to operate on a spectrum. At one end it is fueled by love and is a medium for love. At the other end, it is fueled by desire, a focus on me and mine, and is often agitated.

The heart seeks constancy that can only be found in love. When humangee is awake, love opens the heart; humangee can appreciate the need of the moment and may discern the knowledge needed to meet the need.

For example, compassion allows one to attend to the needs of others without being affected by their suffering.

As we've learned, all of life can be seen as a play, serious or playful. It does not need to be burdensome; it doesn't have to cause misery. One learns to see that which resides in all beings, the essence; seeing life as a play, allows for an open heart. This is a big heart.

Being big-hearted, one lives a big life. In simple terms, the size of our life is the size of our heart.

A Heart with Room to Grow!

Some might say they never got the opportunity to serve. In some situations this may be valid, but in most circumstances the reality is that, with more heart, one gets more power and endurance and becomes awake and open and thus more aware of opportunities to serve.

When you are awake and your heart is open, you are better positioned to handle the difficulties and opportunities that life sets in front of you.

How does a humangee cleanse or open up its heart?

1. **Learn to let go.** Our hearts are naturally pure; they become impure because of what they are identified with or clinging to. Humangee needs to become detached, to let go of what they are attached to.

2. **Accept life: *all of it.*** We can't just look forward to the good stuff and avoid or turn our noses up at the bad stuff. Embrace both with equanimity. You can and will generally benefit more from the bad stuff.

3. **Use reason or intellect to protect the heart.** Examine the contents of your heart. Identify that which is a burden, acknowledge it as unnecessary and of no purpose, and remove it. Forgive. Do not store poison in your heart.

   It's like removing a stone from your shoe. You have to notice the pain, go to the source, find the stone, and remove it. Let it go. In this way, use reason to remove habitual negative emotions. Reason and the heart work well together. So, nourish the heart with reason (more on this in chapter 16).

4. **Appreciate that acquisition of worldly things will not bring peace of mind.** Develop your ability to discriminate, to discern what brings true peace of mind, and be careful in what you aspire to.

5. **Consciously replace the content of your heart with pure emotions.**

For example, where there is anger, hate, and criticism, replace with their alternative—equanimity, love, praise.

6. **Use speech to purify the heart.** Speak the truth and have nothing to do with untruth. Give praise and practice gratitude; look for appropriate occasions to express truth.

7. **Discipline your desires.** Fulfill only those desires that relate to the present, that are within your power to fulfill, and that do not harm others. This gives natural measure to the desire. Cease contemplating your desires.

8. **Embrace Stillness.** The heart goes out to meet the needs of the world, which requires energy. This energy needs to be replenished. To replenish the energy, one must go inside. This is achieved through mindfulness, present moment attention, and meditation.

❚❚

Humangee's True Capacity

Consider a mother and father of two children, who they love dearly. If they have two more children, the love does not diminish; they love them all equally. In the same way, each one of us has the capacity to love the entire universe, but we make the mistake of choosing to give our love only to a spouse, possibly some children, and maybe even a cat. Like the flea trainer, we take this amazing instrument with a colossal capacity and we restrict it because of conditioning and misunderstanding. We then wonder why we are unsatisfied or disappointed with life because we have limited our love and humanity to such a small circle or group.

In a pure state of heart, reflections come and go, and the heart is unmoved by the external physical world. Life will be an expression of love.

Anything is possible in the natural state of the heart. So, restore your heart to its natural state and enjoy your life.

Thoughts to ponder:

Those who have love in their hearts and reason in their minds feed on bliss. But those whose heart says one thing and their mind says another feed on pleasure and pain, for they have not realized love nor unity.

What the mind says in words, the heart says in silence.

Take care of the world and it will take care of you.

The heart is quicker than the mind.

—Inspired by Shane Mulhall

Meditation

Much has been written about meditation in recent years. The term is thrown around loosely. Most people have good intentions of developing a practice but find the discipline and habit difficult to build and maintain. Hence, unless its value and impact are understood and appreciated, it will not be prioritized.

Most do not go through a meditation preparation process. While this is not cumbersome, it serves to instill a level of respect, reverence, and appreciation for the lineage of the practice, which has been shared and passed on with love. It also serves to ensure a proper understanding of the process and a mechanism to follow up afterward, which is helpful.

In one aspect, meditation is like a complete workout for the mind, learning to stay more intrinsically focused, learning to rest in stillness.

One learns to observe the constant chattering and activity of the externally focused mind and develop the discipline of letting it go, not attaching to the thoughts. From this point and practice, a multiplicity of benefits accrue.

One of the key purposes of meditation is largely to build the mental discipline to come into the present. But it delivers many more benefits as well.

There are other ways to build the habit of coming into the present, like prayer, yoga, tai chi, and activities that you find fully engaging. Art, music, and manual activity have also been shown to deliver these benefits.

Some can achieve similar focus and attention on the processes in the body in high-level sports and in other attention-based activities.

While it can be argued that meditation and mindfulness are the best tools, if these aren't available, it is best to start with whatever you have.

So, it's a bit like the question put to the fitness coach: Which exercise is best?

Answer: It's the one that you actually do!

It is the internal investment of effort to counter the default programming and mind habits of our external world. And like the development of any muscle or habit, it does take work and commitment.

Mentally Fit

In one respect, meditation is to the mind what physical exercise is to the body. It's the best way to build the mental muscle to get in and stay in the present.

It is a central exercise discipline and activity that will enable you to become mentally fit. Like physical fitness, the residual effects last all day and into the next. And you get to reap the benefits on a continual basis when you build up the habit and get mentally fit over time.

Physical Training versus Internal Mind Training

Many humangee put a large focus on their body and externally focused mind, whether through traditional education or physical activity. They put a huge investment into their appearance and career.

Conversely, however, they generally invest little in the intrinsic part that has the scope to deliver what they really want in terms of peace, freedom, and joy.

The heart as a medium for love is our real source of passion, motivation, and drive. It is close to our essence and is central to our true nature. It performs best if allowed to operate with true reason in the mind (more on this in chapter 16). From here the being sees and responds to real needs. This is the subject of our next chapter.

Chapter 12
The Importance of Service

Not Just Action but a Way of Thinking

We've established that humangee is on a journey toward refinement and that progress is built largely on service.

Service is one of the key guiding principles for a prosperous, full, abundant, and joyful life.

For humangee, there are two principle lines of work:

1. On oneself
2. With and for others – serving humanity

There are three components to achieving this work. It is deemed by some to be the noblest work that one can undertake: Here, we'll focus on the first one.

1. *Way of Action*   *Service*
2. Way of Devotion   Meditation
3. Way of Knowledge Knowledge

The way of action is the realization and implementation of service.

Over time, service transforms life into an unfolding expression of love, knowledge, and freedom.

It is available to all and is waiting to be released.

Real service is a form of worship or dedication. What makes it so is the motivation, the inner intent. True service is clean and pure, with no strings attached.

Each humangee serves according to their nature.

Everyone depends on everyone else for needs such as food, drink, warmth, air, somewhere to live, clothes, roads, cars, friends, and partners.

It is useful to awaken to the fact that everything serves everything else. That's just how it works. This runs contrary to the prominent view in today's individualistic society: look after number one. Or, alternatively, the country or government owes me a living.

The nature of true service is like a gift. There is absolutely no claim on it, not even the desire for a positive response from the recipient. It is also provided or delivered to the absolute best of one's ability.

The truth is that humangee actually enjoy serving others, if they will just let themselves do it. You are happy to serve your spouse, your kids, your dog.

Service is not servitude. Many confuse service with servitude. The latter is seen as slavery or a low form of work or an objectionable use of one's time. But that view misses the critical point: through service humangee grows, and their world is enlarged.

Universal love (see chapter 14) binds and unites. It leads to harmony, happiness, and the very fullness of service. The service is a core part of the synergy that works and binds all together.

When one sees the essence in all, and the Earth as a connected family, the provision of service simplifies to one essence serving another essence or all others.

The larger your service, the more friends you have.

Simple Service Rule

As householders and workers, we are by definition active people. And with work, home, and other commitments, time availability is often a challenge.

To address this, consider a simple rule: **Every action should be enacted as a service.** Whether cleaning a toilet or serving a customer, your family, or your country. **Every one.**

Every action should be considered as a service

Discover what this does! Whatever the action, let it be a service. It works wonders. Without thinking about the results, simply serve. Something meaningful is achieved with every step. Life is worth living!

There are many forms of sacrifice: material, mental, and spiritual. If a humangee studies hard and undergoes training to fit herself to be useful to the organization, region, or nation, that is sacrifice. If a humangee accumulates wealth honestly and gives that away for the nourishment and prosperity of the community, or the nation, that is sacrifice. In giving it away, they part with all claim to it and surrender it to the recipient. This is an act where the donor and the recipient are, in fact, one and the same.

Sacrifice is a significant concept. At its root, it nourishes, strengthens, and is true service.

In a business environment, if someone works hard producing goods or services to be sold in the wider community and becomes rich, that is good. A need is served and may not have anything to do with greed. But someone who exploits the labor of others for their own pleasure or advantage is acting out of greed. The distinction is simple.

Why Am I Here?

This is a fundamental question, and part of the answer lies in the area of service.

A common scriptural answer, is: **I am here for the family, the nation, and for the whole world.**

This really means that I am here to serve these entities beyond myself.

Baggage and Service

We previously described the concept of baggage that humangee may bring into this world with him/her. In simple terms, it is either good or bad baggage. The good is or was built on the actions for someone else, other than oneself, and with no desire to gain anything from it. The bad baggage is born of actions taken for one's own selfish advantage. This negative baggage is removed by provision of true service over time.

Would You Worship With or Dedicate This Action?

Use this question as a test to clarify whether your service is true service and meets the criteria of good intent and non-attachment.

Providence

All that we have received at the hands of the universe is to be paid back—everything. Anything we receive, we are grateful for. This view varies from the normal impulse to provide and consider only for oneself.

- The impulse to provide for oneself is treacherous. If humangee chooses this route, they may well get what they ask for, but that's it. That's not exactly a true bounty of riches, relative to the abundance of the universe.

- The wise humangee does not focus on the self but chooses to serve, knowing that those who serve are served, those who feed are fed, those who love are loved.

The transformational act of service

THEN   NOW

Wisdom and Service

When humangee becomes refined, the mind is focused and wisdom enters. That's how it works.

The service begins in the physical world. It progresses to opening the heart, enabling opening of the subtle world. Wisdom is the subtle world, on which humangee grows and feeds others.

Why do we not see needs? Given the wondrous nature of humangee and the unity in which we all exist, why is it that we do not see this demonstration of love and service everywhere? Well, you can find it when you look for it, but it could be seen all the more.

Many do not see the needs either because they are too removed from them or, more likely, they are dreaming and just don't see them. They are so busy in their own preoccupied worlds and simply not awake to the needs that surround them. When humangee is in the present moment, the needs will appear.

Whatever You Are Doing, You Are There to Serve

Whether you are in a business, a social organization, at home, at work, at a sporting event, at a social gathering—your opportunity is to meet the occasion appropriately and serve. We have received education, a body, the mind and heart, and also support from our families and societies. All of this comes from the universe. Our role is simply to repay in the form of service.

Nature is balanced and all is in harmony. The best thing you can do is to provide service without looking for recognition. The whole universe operates on giving and receiving. What disrupts the creation is just taking, particularly when there is no effort or intent to give back.

With regard to service, the body is limited but the mind is not. When humangee searches for truth, it spreads to others. Devoted service can raise the community and engender a new birth or renaissance in the world at large.

Who or What Shall I Serve?

When we hear of this concept of service, many wonder, what can I do to serve? It's like the child in the kitchen who asks, "What do you want me to do?" You could tell them, but this is a short-term solution that doesn't address a long-term opportunity. If they have lived in the same house for years and know where everything goes, then they have the opportunity to take initiative. The opportunity is to see what needs to be done and get on with it. Always asking what needs to be done requires delegation of responsibility.

In the same way, the opportunity for humangee is to be present and awake. In that state, the needs will start to become more apparent. The question then becomes, which need should be served?

The Task

There is an opportunity to grow in refinement and wisdom through proper study and to serve the community or nation in enlightening and practical ways. The perfection of wisdom is such that one knows one's essence. Knowing one's own essence, one knows everyone else's. Wisdom brings unity. Humangee can resolve to make our actions gradually more lawful and natural, until all the separateness has gone.

Serving with Pleasure and Ease

The next thing that arises for humangee from this physical service is this: whatever one serves fully, without limitation or restraint, one becomes devoted to, and love arises in the heart.

Service in this state, taking place in love, is devoid of effort and done with pleasure, delight, and extraordinary ease. This arises naturally and appeals to and strengthens the devotional part of humangee.

If we love the service in some way or another, then all sense of burden and duty goes out of it, resulting in a remarkable change. Think of the young mother who loves to care for her child, not out of duty but with pleasure. We get more by serving more.

Dedication

A key principle across all the disciplines and practices is the dedication of our actions and service to something greater than the self. That could be the universe, unity, God, an absolute, or any other reference one chooses to allocate.

It is based on a guiding principle that the greater can satisfy the lesser, but the lesser cannot satisfy the greater.

So, this suggests that having a focus on something greater or doing something for the wider good serves us all. This could be family, club, nation, profession, or world.

If your life is in service to unity, or a teacher or an ideal, or to truth itself, that is the best service. It makes ALL the difference to the service.

How we treat others, especially those in need, tells us something about ourselves.

Our neighbor is not only one of us, but could be anyone, anywhere.

In practicing charity, consider the following:

» It is better to give privately or in secret rather than publicly.
» It benefits the giver as much, if not more than, the receiver.
» It should be more of a commitment than simply giving from what you have left over.
» Being in a position of financial comfort is a gift, that is not entirely within our control, and should thus be shared.
» Consider that hoarding and depriving others has the same net effect as stealing.
» Our brothers and sisters should not be deprived from living a dignified life.
» Charity is the love of unity, love of neighbor, and love of self.

Charity Is a Form of Service

Almsgiving. Sadaqah. Zakath. Altruism.

Charity is a clear, unambiguous expression of love, and extends beyond simply goodwill and benevolence in how we treat others.

Charity is not:

» optional for a humangee, but an essential aspect
» a guilty handful of coins, begrudgingly given
» a pang of consciousness

Chapter 13

Responsibility: The Ability to Respond

The term *responsibility* for many people is a subjective word. It can be perceived in different ways by different people in different circumstances. A traditional definition might be: something that you have a job or duty to deal with. But in its simplest sense, it is the ability to respond—to a person, an event, a role, and in the widest sense to a need.

The following chapter sets out that responsibility is a core principle that builds on our capacity to respond. This includes self-responsibility, a duty to look after yourself, and then grows to a small group like a family or a community. In the truest sense of the word, we all have a responsibility to each other, our countries, our universe—to all that is.

This truth is succinctly summarized in the biblical command to love our neighbor as ourselves.

All humangee have the opportunity to fully understand and accept their response-ability. However, generations of humangee have struggled to pass on the true concept to those coming after them. Today, people tend to take full responsibility only for those very close to themselves. Some humangee believe they are really only responsible for themselves and possibly a small circle of people around them. And worse, many defer their responsibility, insisting that others are responsible for them: their government, their employer,

their local council. They take little responsibility for themselves or anyone else.

It may sound ludicrous, but this lack of responsibility is a mindset virus that is widespread in our world. It is responsible for a wide range of issues from racial and religious separation to climate and ecosystem indifference. From hoarding of wealth to unwillingness to help others. It scales up to national and international levels. It is at the source of every evil and problem at every level in our society.

What Is a Well-Functioning Humangee Responsible For?

Self-Responsibility

What are we responsible for?

We are masters of ourselves.

> The following is adapted from James Allen's *As a Man Thinketh*:
>
> As a being of power, intelligence, and love, a person's own state is within their power and is their responsibility. Lord of his own thoughts, humangee holds the key to every situation—to make of himself what he wills.
>
> As humangee, we are created; as individuals we are self-made.
>
> We are responsible for our body, mind, and heart, and thus for our actions, thoughts, and feelings.

Hence, we are responsible for the consequences of what we feel, think and do. While this may seem difficult, we are free to choose ALL of the time.

We own the choice on how we respond to any given circumstance. Nobody can take away this freedom, but we can choose not to exercise it.

We may feel powerless in relation to what is happening in our lives, but the power to choose how to respond is ours, whether with love, compassion, anger, frustration, hurt, guilt, or something else.

If we harbor love, hatred, jealousy—like attracts like.

As a person thinketh in his heart, so are they. We are literally what we think.

Under various laws an input generates an output. Take gravity, for example: if something is held above the ground, when released, it falls according to that law. The same applies to the actions of humangee, where the key variable is often the time from input to output. Hence, how a person or humangee manifests is an unfolding or consequence under law.

A selfish, irresponsible and evil person is the product of sustained engagement of ignorant thoughts. A principled and good person is the outcome of sustained effort and natural, correct thinking. The time scale is not specified.

In the context of mind and heart, know that good thoughts or beliefs bear good fruit and bad ones bear bad fruit. On this basis, humangee are made or unmade by themselves.

Having the power to choose our thoughts, we are ultimately the molders of our character, the makers and shapers of our environment and destiny.

We are the reapers of our own harvest. We are not slaves to the tyranny of circumstance.

Humankind is manacled only by themselves. Their wishes and prayers are only gratified when they harmonize with their words and actions.

Humangee's innermost thoughts and desires are fed with their own food, whether it be foul or clean.

Not what a person wishes and prays for do they get, but what they justly earn.

People manacle themselves

Collective Responsibility

This is a concept that crosses some people's radar, but sadly not all. The fact is, as individuals we are not islands; we are totally connected to everybody else.

Whether we like it or not, we are all involved in everything that happens in the whole world—directly or indirectly. So there is nothing anywhere that we are not responsible for. This may seem like a sweeping statement, but is worth reflection.

Everything in the universe is connected. This is reflected clearly in the many inequalities across the world at present. These range from the extremes of wealth at one end to the extremes of poverty, injustice, deprivation, and human suffering at the other. And until there is a wider waking up to this collective irresponsibility and duality, then progress to resolve it will continue to be slow.

Kahlil Gibran explains it elegantly in "On Crime and Punishment":[5]

> Oftentimes have I heard you speak of one who commits a wrong as though he were not one of you, but a stranger unto you and an intruder upon your world.
>
> But I say that even as the holy and righteous cannot rise beyond the highest which is in each one of you,
>
> So the wicked and the weak cannot fall lower than the lowest which is in you also.
>
> And as a single leaf turns not yellow but with the silent knowledge of the whole tree,
>
> So the wrongdoer cannot do wrong without the hidden will of you all.

> Like a procession you walk together toward your god-self.
>
> You are the way and the wayfarers.
>
> And when one of you falls down, he falls for those behind him, a caution against the stumbling stone.
>
> Ay, and he falls for those ahead of him, who though faster and surer of foot, yet removed not the stumbling stone.

Consider that phrase, "a single leaf turns not yellow but with the silent knowledge of the whole tree." It reflects that every wrongdoer does so with the hidden will of us all.

Even if we believe that we are not responsible *for* others, do we accept that we are responsible *to* others?

There is a need to be awake to our collective responsibility and aware of simply turning a blind eye because we are too busy surviving. This becomes obvious to those who are open enough to see. It helps explain our failures on equality, gender, poverty, and more.

Lack of Responsibility

The key fundamental limiting thought is my identity, my ego, who I think I am. Hence if we continue with this logic, then the following emerges:

- If I think I'm an individual, then I'm responsible to and for myself, and no one else.
- If I think I'm a family man or woman then I'm responsible to and for my family, but no one else's.

---

5 Kahlil Gibran, "On Crime and Punishment," poets.org, accessed October 13, 2020, https://poets.org/poem/crime-and-punishment.

- If I think I'm an Italian then I'm responsible for Italians and anything Italian.
- If I think I'm a human being then I'm responsible for all of humanity.
- If I think I'm essence then I am and feel that I am responsible to and for ALL.

This position then clarifies other consequences. We know that other than essence or spirit, any identity when taken seriously hardens our hearts.

When our hearts are hardened, it's impossible for us to respond fully. We react in three possible ways to the world around us:

- That which I love/like, I respond to.
- That which I dislike, I react benignly, malignly to.
- That which I am indifferent to, I do not respond to.

The implication is that most people respond to a very small proportion of the universe. We may not think that the consequences are accumulating, but they are.

Impact of Lack of Responsibility

With limited or erroneous thoughts filling our minds, we firmly believe in "injustice." We become angered by the injustices by, to,

and from other people. We feel ourselves to be badly treated.

We then grumble or get irritated at the state of the world. Or, having accepted injustices in our lives, we accept them in the lives of others. Does this resonate with you?

Distinguishing Reaction and Response

Reaction and habits reflect our failing to respond or to be responsible. We identify with our body, its sensations, and its mind, heart, and feelings. These identifications limit us and we react. It's as mechanical as turning on a light switch. For example, when we say someone is pushing our buttons or pulling our strings, it's an indication of the ways we are so attached to our ego identity.

People insult us, make us angry, sad, and annoyed. Someone can praise us and make us feel valued, worthy, and happy.

However, whether insult or praise, these are in principle both the same in that we react to them. We become puppets to inputs from other people. In this state we cannot control or manage our minds and hearts.

Taking Things Personally

Other people and factors of our environment control us. We have developed an ego that takes everything personally. And it is this unseen monster that makes us react.

We might perceive that everyone else's reactions are over the top, but ours are reasonable and justified. And as a result of reaction and not response, we do not see what is truly in front of us and what is really happening.

In this state, every action has the force that makes it repeated again, again, and again. As a result, we cut channels in our emotional hearts, thus developing mental and emotional grooves and chains.

The result over time is that we can only behave in a certain way. The more we act in these predictable ways, the more they are reinforced. These reactions then have a lease over our life. That's it, for our entire life. Unless we wake up.

Have you ever considered that in some aspects you could be living parts of your life as a puppet to your mind?

Who or what pulls your strings?

Possessed by Our Habits

These reactions are self-perpetuating; everything is done simply by force of habit. Even the mind that does not agree with the action, even the heart that is troubled by it—they are compelled to carry it out.

We regret the unconscious action immediately after, but that does not stop us from doing it again and again. Habit forces us to do things, and we become their victim.

Basically, we live through our habits, or our habits live through us. Habits become our masters, and we become their servants. It's like being possessed. Our habits become our first nature, and our true nature becomes secondary.

These habits are the reactions of our accumulated past. **The presence of reaction means absence of response-ability.**

These reactions manifest emotionally as anger, pessimism, irritability, despondency, complaining, or as condemning and grumbling.

The world of reactions is one of divisions— quarrelling, wars, litigation, accusation, foolishness, and hatred.

When we are subject to these, then we are subject to injustice because we cannot help but see injustice.

Is there no injustice in this world?

The humangee of reaction sees injustice everywhere. The person of responsibility sees the operation of justice at work in every aspect of life.

The "sense of injustice" is the fruit of the reaction and is real to the reactionary. We see injustices in the actions of others because we see only the immediate appearances. We regard every act to stand

---

107

by itself, independent of the law of cause and effect. We judge on the basis of the effect only, not knowing the cause.

However, as you sow, so shall you reap. The invisible law is operating all the time, everywhere. But mainly unseen and rarely believed in.

Anger

Anger is one of the most common forms of reaction. When we get angry, we say we are doing it. We rationalize it, saying that the situation demanded it. I had to be angry, otherwise the other person would have got away with some wrong or would have trampled over me.

Anger NEVER comes out of the current situation. We are always angry with the wrong person. Read that again: anger never comes out of the current situation. We are not angry with the person right in front of us. This anger comes out of the past, which is stored either on your hard drive or cloud storage archive. It is stored in your being from past events and interpretations.

If you didn't store anger in your being, how could you get angry now? When you look properly, you will find that you are just living off your stored reserves of anger. And some unfortunate individual in front of you is paying for it in the present.

That poor pedestrian, casually walking across your junction, looking at their mobile phone—they become a subject of anger as you toot the horn or vent the irritation you've bottled inside. But it's nothing to do with them.

We're not angry because of that thing our husband, wife, partner just said to us. They have simply supplied an occasion for anger or given us the possibility to be angry.

You make me so angry!

But the anger was there already waiting for the opportunity to express itself. Had it not expressed itself with your spouse, it would have been with someone else, at another time.

So, all that anger that you have stored inside of you has to express itself someday! For, as you may now be starting to see, nothing in nature is hidden forever.

It's worth reflecting on what anger or frustration is hiding in the cupboards of your mind. When one truly sits back and observes the world of reaction, we realize how stupid it really is.

When you are awake and removed from the circumstances, one sees human reactions for the comedy or tragedy show that they are.

Becoming Response-able

How then do we become responsible? Consider the following practices. Some of the following will seem very blunt, challenging, and unrealistic. Reflect on those you find thought-provoking or that grate against your current beliefs. Test them in practical day-to-day living to see if they start to make sense to you.

1. Letting go

We should let go of all desires,[6] claims, and attachments.

Do not give them any admittance into your heart. When they present themselves, let them pass without reacting to them or acting on them.

2. Self-restraint

Develop self-restraint and check or control negative emotions and invalid desires. Resist temptations and unhelpful desires. Guard yourself against unuseful tendencies.

The intelligent way to check against unuseful desires is to refer to an ideal/a teacher (e.g., how would Krishna, Jesus, Muhammad, Lao Tzu, Socrates, or your chosen ideal respond to this?). Adapt this as a standard. Restraint alone will not dissolve reactions. To dissolve reactions, we must purify our hearts.

3. Empathy

Without empathy, we must be prejudiced. Prejudice kills kindness, love, sympathy, and true judgment.

In practicing empathy, we understand the ignorance of others. The fruit of prejudice is hatred toward others.

With empathy, compassion arises for the ignorance in others. We enter fully into their hearts and lives, not burdened with the badness in others, we then uplift our neighbor. With compassion, useful action follows.

So, we should strive mentally to put ourselves in the place of others, drawing out the goodness in them. Then instead of judging harshly and reacting to them, we will understand them by entering into their experience. In understanding them, we can respond in love to their need.

This is the fulfillment of the great principle, "Do onto others as you would have them do unto you."

Mankind has a great freedom—the ability to choose their emotional state in any situation. No doubt this seems challenging. When we are fully present, we can observe the emotions but not be engulfed by them, attached to them, or identify with them.

But due to ignorance, ordinarily we react. These reactions produce all the negative emotions, such as irritation, hatred, greed, anger, vanity, pride, envy.

We can or could choose instead to respond with patience, love, compassion, curiosity, self-sacrifice, fearlessness, and humility. Reacting only compounds the problem.

---

6   The specific definition of the term *desire* used in this book is clarified in Chapter 15.

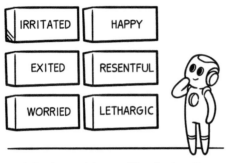

What would you like today?

❚❚

4. Raising others up

When you are wronged, do not get even. Rather, make the other person even (i.e., equal to us). Love them, forgive them. To initiate a change often requires an insti- gator—someone who breaks the pattern, someone who is open to trusting these principles and doing what is actually right rather than reacting to an event. Being awake gives you the choice to break a cycle and uplift another. Raise the other up. Raise them to ourselves. Live by example.

Getting even simply reduces both parties. Making the other person even raises both parties. By raising yourself to your highest level through your loving response, you raise the other also.

Remember, there is no beneficiary to negative emotions. Both giver and receiver suffer.

> **Confucius:** The fruit of negative feelings is endless misery and suffering.
>
> It is helpful to reflect deeply on this to ensure we appreciate its veracity.

A practice to consider: Before reacting, ask the question, "What is the highest, best, most loving response that I can give to this person or situation?" You have the option to give it.

In this way we respond from the divine in us rather than reacting from the animal within us.

5. Acceptance

Every time we react, life has won—we have lost.

The events of life do not destroy a person. They only show what we are made of at that moment in time.

The turmoil of the world we may not be able to avoid, but the turmoil of our mind is of our own choosing.

Our life is perfect for us right now. Stop seeking change. The first thing to accept is life—all of it.

If we can bring about this conviction, we will respond fully to our lives. Make use of the bad and the good that befalls us. Then instead of allowing the bad to limit us or bring us down, it will simply help us grow. In truth, nothing good or bad happens to us. It is all for our education.

Life is a school: Are we reacting or respond- ing? It is an opportunity for us to grow, to learn the truth about ourselves. Are we learning?

Everything that irritates you in another person is actually telling you something about yourself, something that needs working on.

> So, when you say, "That person really gets to me," that is telling you something about yourself, not them. It's showing you something you need to consider in yourself, and possibly review or work on.

▮▮

Meet everyone as if they were your teacher—and let them teach you. It may be that they will teach you about patience, forgiveness, or compassion. Another particularly useful practice is to see and experience every person you meet as if it were for the first time.

6. Capacity

What capacity do we have for responsibility, for love, for wisdom, for serving? What is the capacity of a humangee?

It is not only for testing our qualities that one needs to take responsibility but also for finding our shortcomings. Accept responsibility for identifying your shortcomings.

Do not be afraid of letting your highest possibilities shine. So, don't be afraid of being number one. Accept responsibility for your talents and for their full glorious manifestation. If we hide our light under a bushel, we simply make the world a darker place.

There is no such thing as a role without responsibility. Therefore, we must accept responsibility for our talents and chosen work.

With capacity comes responsibility: As a nurse or doctor, we cannot refuse to help the ill. Whatever roles we play are accompanied by responsibility.

Husband is responsible for wife, and wife is responsible for husband. If you are married, do you see yourself as responsible for the welfare and happiness of your spouse?

Employers are responsible for employees, and employees are responsible for employers.

Government is responsible for its citizens, and citizens are also responsible for their government.

This applies for all tribes, groups, and collectives.

We always have more capacity for these natural attributes of responsibility, love, service, and wisdom.

▮▮

7. Contentment

Be content with your friends, family, spouse, children, and work—now. Accept whatever has happened up to now. Do not aim to be content in the future. Be content now. This doesn't preclude action to change a situation.

To permit true contentment, it is permissible not to be content with three things:
- Our understanding
- Our character
- Our spiritual unfoldment

These always have room for refinement.

How can we become responsible?

To become responsible, we accept responsibility for ourselves and our internal lives.

The first thing we do is stop blaming others. We stop blaming the past, the government, our background, etc.

Initially this may seem quite depressing as we consider our present state and learn to accept total responsibility for it. But this passes in time and is soon replaced by a great sense of freedom and strength. We can now determine our own lives.

How others behave and how the world unfolds leaves us untouched because we are willing to be the masters of ourselves. And this awareness of choice restores our free will to us.

Transforming ourselves by being responsible

to

Thought to ponder:

We can transform the world if we transform ourselves.

8. Self-inquiry

There is a need for real self-inquiry. Thoroughly examine the contents and the working of your mind and remove or disempower that which does not stand to reason.

To be free of reaction and thus be responsible, the mind needs true knowledge. Therefore, false knowledge needs to be rooted out. It is this false knowledge that causes reaction.

To help ourselves become responsible, we should ask real, genuine questions of the mind:

Who is my neighbor?

What is my duty to my fellow humangee?

Do I have the right to choose to love one and not another?

In order to have true knowledge, there is a need to practice discrimination or discernment. Opinions and thoughts should all be questioned. That which is believed should be tested.

The fixed ideas of *I am right* or *I know* need to be dropped so that there is total openness. It would be better for us to ask, *Am I right?* or *Is this true?*

Then whatever we believe in, we act upon. If we do not believe in something, we will not act on it.

So, our beliefs need to be examined, and if they do not stand up to reason or practice, they should be dropped.

If we are prone to harshly condemn or judge others, we should look within and see to what degree we fall short.

> Confucius taught that any fool can see faults in others and the goodness in himself, but it takes wisdom to see the goodness in others and the faults in oneself.

Over time, the wise have taught that evil is overcome only by good. Yet how often do we try to overcome evil with evil, anger with anger, competition with aggression?

This principle needs to be learned. No longer can we meet mistrust with mistrust and skepticism, and negativity with cynicism, resistance, and negativity.

The universal principle—you reap what you sow—leads us to a responsible life.

9. Resolution

To move from reaction to response, resolution is essential. The power of habit is so strong that without a firm irrevocable decision, no substantial work can be accomplished.

So, uncovering the reactionary aspects of our lives and becoming dissatisfied with them, we take action.

Resolution arises when you appreciate a need and commit yourself to deal with it fully and properly.

Half-hearted or premature resolution is no resolution at all. We probably already know that hasty or shallow commitments simply do not work.

So, we should be slow to make resolutions. They should be the result of deep examination and full understanding.

On making a resolution, ALL the force of habit will rise to test the commitment. The determination and resolve must be firm.

The idea is that once a true resolution is made, it is **never abandoned.** Be slow to make resolutions or binding commitments.

> **James Allen, *As a Man Thinketh***[7]
>
> "Man's mind may be likened to a garden, which may be intelligently cultivated or allowed to run wild; but whether cultivated or neglected, it must, and will, *bring forth*. If no useful seeds are *put* into it, then an abundance of useless weed-seeds will *fall* therein, and will continue to produce their kind.
>
> Just as a gardener cultivates his plot, keeping it free from weeds, and growing the flowers and fruits which he requires, so may a man tend the garden of his mind, weeding out all the wrong, useless, and impure thoughts, and cultivating toward perfection the flowers and fruits of right, useful, and pure thoughts."

What are the flowers and fruits of right, useful, and pure thoughts? Are we the master gardeners of our mind, or has the garden been allowed to run wild?

Have we weeded out that which is counterproductive to our happiness, peace, freedom, and love?

---

7   James Allen, *As a Man Thinketh*, CreateSpace, 2006.

The Parable of the Talents

Original Parable of the Talents:

This is an important and subtle parable that is intended to demonstrate our responsibility simply to use what the universe has given us!

In the Bible, Jesus tells the story of a rich man who has three servants. He gives each servant an amount of money, referred to as talents, based upon that man's ability to steward and care for the money. The first steward is given five talents, the second is given two talents, and the third is given one. The master tells them to care for his money and the first two servants use the talents to trade and gain profit. They return to their master with double the talents. The third servant is fearful and hides the one talent he was trusted with, returning just one talent to his master. The master is angry and scolds him, saying that he should have invested or used the money to make it grow.

Consider the parable of the talents as a guide story to encourage and challenge us to take what has been given to us in our life and invest and add value to the universe. There is great reward waiting for those who steward well what the universe has given them.

It doesn't matter what one is given or what one starts with. All that is important is that we do the best we can with the hand we have been dealt.

The somewhat less well-known Story of the Three Humangee:

To give the humangee population some feedback, an experiment was conducted in which three humangee reported how they fared during their lives, recording what they made of what they had been given.

Alex was born into a well-off environment and was artistic.

Sam was raised in a modest family environment and given many talents, including being very smart.

Jas was born into a poor environment and was given a talent to be a musician.

Each had the opportunity to take their talents out into the world and see what they could do.

Alex excelled in school and also discovered she had artistic talents. She was interested in money and chose to go into business. And while she found some success, much of her focus was on accumulating material things. While others deemed her to be successful, she lived a primarily unhappy and unfulfilled life, never awakening and discovering little overall progression.

Sam had what was deemed a good family background, was uninterested at school, and left quite young. She never encountered a mentor and rarely found opportunities to wake up. She did not get to appreciate her real talents and fell into some bad habits. Sam died relatively young in a car crash, due to not paying attention. Hers was not a particularly happy or progressive life.

Jas had little to do as a youth and discovered she had a talent for music. She spent hours refining and developing her skill. One day she joined an orchestra and over time got the opportunity to share her gift with audiences around the world, getting paid for the privilege. She came to appreciate the universal laws and exercised a joyous, content life.

**It's about doing what you can
to make the best of what you've got**

Key takeaways:

- What you start with is of low relevance.
- The key difference is what you do with what you are given.
- Particularly with regard to the inner realm, live an awakened life rather than one that remains in sleep.
- Humangee is discontent to the extent that they resist their current reality.
- If you are awake, things generally work out better for you.

True responsibility starts with self-responsibility, which is largely a function of being awake and present.

We then appreciate who and what we are responsible for. Being responsible for oneself sets the foundation for our ability to serve others, from our family to our community and beyond. We also learn to see the consequences of not being responsible to self and others.

On being responsible for self and others, we have the scope to be responsible for all, which is a foundation for love in its truest sense.

Chapter 14
Love and Emotions

What Is Love?

Love is the core emotion from which all other emotions emanate. It is a foundational component of the inner being; everyone has pure love within their nature. In the same way that all have an essence or soul, we have heart which is the medium for love. It may not always seem apparent, but it exists as an inherent natural attribute.

As a natural force, love is deemed to be the underlying force of desire for unity, where two become one. Thus the perception of duality is replaced by unity—we see ourselves in others and them in us.

It is part of every person's true nature to be full of wisdom, happiness, and love. It is centered in the emotional heart.

A Single Word for a Deep Concept

The lexicon in English for the full range of aspects of love is limited relative to other languages. There are a range of different feelings and experiences all described by the word *love*. There are over twenty descriptions given in a standard dictionary, which convey a wide range of scenarios and contexts. The word is both a verb and a noun. It applies to things, activities, aspirations, outcomes: to be in love, to love swimming, love songs and love stories.

Many songs relate to the effects of love on the mind, apparently often resulting in erratic behavior: blinded by love, pained by love, falling in love, and being crazy in love.

Suffice to say that the word is widely and loosely used, with a limited or specific appreciation of the true nature of the emotion.

In Greek philosophy there are three aspects of love, of another person or thing considered. These are:

1. **Eros** signifies intense desire or passion.
2. **Philia** refers to friendship, or a brotherly or sisterly form of love for a smallish group.
3. **Agape** is universal love. This would include the love that someone may have for the whole world or the whole of mankind, irrespective of personalities, race, or creed.

It is useful to explore these three aspects on a personal and practical level to cultivate an understanding of the distinction.

It is a foundation for ensuring appropriate love for self, love for another, love for a small group—like family or extended family or community—and a wider agape-type love for the whole universe.

In this manual, the premise put forward is that agape is the highest and truest form of love.

Love Is the Primary Emotion

1. Love is the singular emotion from which all other emotions emanate. This is explained or clarified further in the section below.
2. An additional aspect, which the wise have reiterated over time, is "Everyone has pure love within their nature, and all strive to express this love through the creation."

These are two big statements, which many readers will no doubt struggle with.

Practical philosophy dissects these assertions, holding them up to the test of personal experience in order to examine their validity. Not in theory or in hypothetical scenarios, but in your personal life experience.

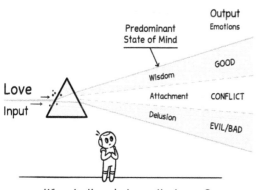

Why do they behave that way?

Consider the diagram, which depicts a prism. In nature when light shines through a translucent object, the spectrum of light is formed. You'll see it in a physics lab or in a rainbow.

In this case, the light of love is the only source going in. It is the primary emotion. And like a spectrum that emanates from the prism, a full spectrum of emotions emanates from humangee/human. These emotions are then determined or influenced by the state of the being's mind and heart.

> In a heart that lives by the laws and operates under wisdom, the net outputs are good and pure.
>
> **In a heart and mind pulled by duality and attachments,** the outputs are conflict and dissonance.
>
> **In a heart and mind that is deluded,** the resulting outcome is bad, evil, and destructive.
>
> **In this way, while pure love is the source, the state of the mind, heart, and body manifest the thoughts, words, and actions.**

Qualities of pure or true love:

- Eternal, forgiving, limitless, immutable, and unchanging.
- Everyone is impelled by love.
- Happiness comes from loving more so than being loved.
- Love does not bargain.
- Where there is true love, there is no fear.
- True love accepts you totally and without judgment.
- Love does not cause grief, only attachments.
- Preferences of one over another undermines love.
- There is a need to distinguish love in the subtle world from that in the gross (body/physical) world.

- The giving of love is its own reward and is never wasted.
- Is not dependent on circumstances.

What is it that we love? What is the object of our love?

Trying to understand what it is that we love in a person or thing helps clarify the potentially shallow perceptions and divide true love from surface attractions.

True love is constant.

When someone expresses love for a person, what is the object of love?

- Is it the physical body, the appearance, the clothes, the eau de cologne?
- Is it the way a person behaves, their demeanor, or their sense of humor?
- Is it the way a person thinks, or the things we believe that we have in common?
- Is it the way a person feels or makes me feel?
- Or is it something more subtle, like their essence, their inner being?

The first four are transient, the last one is permanent.

If love is only true if it's pure and permanent, then we should aim to get a better understanding of the real emotion we are experiencing, if it is not true love.

Limited and Unlimited Love

It is important to distinguish two types of love: when love is unlimited or when love is limited.

When it is limited or restricted, this could be deemed duality and is covered in the following section. It is contrary to seeing yourself in all.

Limited Love as the Basis for Duality and Hostility

If love is so powerful, and if it is natural, why is there so much evil, hatred, and division in the world? What are the causes of this conundrum? What gives rise to this duality?

As mentioned above, our perception of love may not always be correct. When humangee desires a thing it believes it loves, hostility often results if the desire is not satisfied. This often brings to light the incomplete love at the root of the desire.

While love supports and sustains every humangee in the world, this limited love is the cause of hostility (see prism diagram).

Hence it is useful to understand the nature of this duality of love and hostility so that we may have some hope of addressing the irritations, frustrations, misunderstandings, and miscommunications that often come up.

Where there is duality of love, it is incomplete. We uphold an us-and-them dynamic. A love free from this duality is true love.

Duality—ignoring the unity—manifests the effects of seeing anyone as other than oneself.

Notice this at work in the seemingly innocuous separation of groups. For example, family circles, communities of interest, support groups, competitive teams, nations. It's my gang versus the other gang—us and them.

Limiting the Love to a Group

Love is often limited to a smaller group whereby those included are accepted or loved but those outside are not. The group may be made up of the individual or friends, families, social groups, religious groups, racial or ethnic groups, or nations.

While there is nothing intrinsically wrong with any of these groups, the error comes when they are seen as the limit or extent of love and not the basis for expansion into wider love.

For example, love of one's family or friends is natural. But what happens when the love stops at that group of friends? It may just become insular. Sometimes "my" friends are loved but another group is regarded as a threat in some way. It is not long before the groups **start focusing on the differences** and the gangs start fighting each other. All this is due to love being limited to a small group or circle.

What does it feel like to be excluded from any such group?

■■

The Natural Expansion of a Child's Love

Alternatively, consider when a child is born. For the first few years the limit of the child's love is the family, and in particular the mother. As the child grows and then goes to school, the love may expand to include teachers, friends and so on. Later, this may continue to expand. A person may come to love the community in which he or she lives.

That may grow to include one's country and even the whole of humanity.

Where love is exclusive, it excludes others, it stops this natural process of expansion. The exclusivity creates a group, which is fixed and rigid. Beyond the group there may be indifference, which can easily turn into hatred. Even within the tribe, the so-called love can turn sour. The expansion of love is thus reduced by all kinds of jealousies, desires, and aversions. Hence conflicts arise within the group.

Thus, limiting the love to a group or circle creates duality both within it and outside it.

The Concept of Other

For example, anyone outside the groups we have been considering may be regarded as "other," as different from oneself. This may manifest as anything from polite indifference to hatred.

Are there any people whom you personally regard as *other*? More than one, perhaps?

This concept of *other* can operate across all the groups and between nations, race, and religions. When the sense of other becomes strong, it results in duality and hostility and even persecution and war.

119

What is the effect on us when someone or some group regards us or treats us as other, as separate from him or her or that group? How does that affect our feelings and actions?

Alternatively, what is the effect when we are included?

Observe that there may be natural groups or circles. A loving humangee sits across and above these groupings and is not limited.

A pure, true natural humangee has choices and enables others to see that they too have choices to not restrict their love to an exclusive group.

The Potter: Discipline and Love

Are love and discipline two separate and possibly even opposed things? Discipline is thought to require focus and commitment and be difficult to maintain.

We can also see it in the context of what some call "tough love." The receiver may not see the giver's actions or attitudes as loving at the time, but the intent is ultimately for their best good. Some might even perceive it as having nothing to do with love but as depriving them of freedom and happiness. Tough love is true love, as it pains the giver more than the receiver.

Love might be considered as an escape from or an alternative to discipline. Do you recognize any of these perceptions within yourself?

Let us consider love and discipline based on wisdom.

On this basis, they are not opposed to each other. **They mutually support each other.** Without such balance, love is liable to lose its direction and its purity.

Without love, discipline based on wisdom may become hard and even cruel. But when both are present in proper measure, they strengthen and support each other.

The Potter

Consider the potter using clay to throw a pot.

She starts with a blob of malleable clay, a being in control of what she assists to create.

The potter's wheel starts turning slowly. One hand pushes from above, into the center, while the other holds, controls, and caresses the clay to determine its shape.

Both hands are used, one inside and the other outside. The hand inside is the hand of love, which gives support and guidance for expansion. The hand on the outside is the hand of discipline, which ensures that the expansion takes place in the desired and measured way. Together it is both balanced and beautiful.

The growth and development of the being is like the clay of the pot. Both hands are necessary and play a vital part, a **hand of love and a hand of discipline.**

If the love aspect dominates, the expansion is too great and the pot becomes thin in places and can break.

If discipline is too strong, the being does not expand and thrive the way that it could and becomes an imbalanced shell of its true self.

Appropriate discipline and love are especially important for children—young humangee—but the idea applies to many relationships, including teaching, parenting, tutoring, coaching, and more.

Both Love and Discipline...

To mold and realize a true humangee requires two hands, one of love and one of discipline

Impediments to Love

What things, paradigms, beliefs, or perceptions reduce our capacity to love or experience love from another? Some of these will seem counter to what we have been led to believe or may require investigation.

1. The concept of preferences

How does a child develop a preference to Saturday? Does it have to withdraw its preference for Monday? Before they understood the concept of preference, the child loved every day equally. In a life without preferences, likes, and dislikes, we observe the full variety available for us to delight in. Every preference that arises in **this wider context** is a burden to the heart.

Give up your preferences and you'll love everything again. Preferences destroy love.

Without preferences exists a life of steady contentment—happiness.

⏸

2. Love is misdirected

It is turned from the subtle world to the gross, external world. The imbalanced pursuit of pleasure results primarily in pain. This is expanded on and explained in more detail in the next chapter on desire.

3. Possessions and attachments

The extent to which we are dominated by possessions, unnecessary acquisition and retention of things, and external experiences is a reflection of our capacity to love.

Love does not cause grief, it's our attachments or possessions that give rise to our pain. Possessing, acquiring, and achieving do not set you free, but love and freedom go hand in hand.

Misconceptions

There are a number of misconceptions, myths, and trite comments or sayings about love. A few of these are outlined below.

- **Love has a limit.** Not so. Does the mother of four children have less love to go around than the mother of three?
- **Love can be wasted.** Not the case. It is never wasted.
- **Love has a beginning (and hence, an end).** Again, not the case. If so, when did it actually start?
- **You need two to love.** False. The capacity to love others is dependent only on the love of yourself. (Only need one to love.)
- **In love, opposites attract.** In short, this argument does not stand up to scrutiny.
- **Love weakens you.** Not the case. A practical example may clarify whether it was love or not, limited or unlimited. To "fall in love" is either infatuation, lust, or one of the four temporary forms mentioned earlier.

These are concise reflections. Test them for yourself in real-world practice, when truly awake or with someone on the journey of awakening.

While a love may not initially be true, it is possible for it to become so over time, with an opening of the heart and refinement of the being.

Love All with a Capital L

Shifting to the paradigm of loving all is a big jump for many humangee.

When you tell your partner, "I love you," how do they react? Positively, I suspect. Or depending on the maturity of the relationship, you may get a look that conveys, "What have you done now?" ☺

If you then say, "But I love Joe (or Joan) next door too," what's the response? You can add, "I love our whole family. In fact, I love the whole planet." Your sanity may be called into question.

If we have a deeper appreciation of the true meaning of love, all humangee are one family on the same planet. One household. Why would we choose to love one over another? We shouldn't.

Then the specific love for those that are close to us develops a new and refined dimension. It is not based on looks or physical attributes. You make a choice to love the whole essence of this person or thing.

The possibility and intention to live from a place of love opens up new vistas.

Distinguish love for the inner from love for the outer. It is possible to love all, but not like all. You may encounter some who exhibit behaviors or aspects you may not find agreeable. It's a case of you love the essence but not the form. Love the inner but acknowledge the outer.

Some thoughts for a humangee to ponder to help the paradigm of true love take hold:

- Live love and gratitude.
- Be present and awake as often as you can, and see, feel, and touch the beauty all around.
- Consider replacing your fearful or irritated thoughts with compassionate and loving ones.
- Today is a great day to excel and express your love for self and others.
- True discipline is love of self.
- Love for self, love for family and community, love for all, love for planet.
- When one looks for life's perfection, it is often found.
- Take nothing for granted.
- To love and serve, ask: What needs done, right now?
- More than a body and mind, the essence or soul should be the central focus of one's life.
- Cultivate love for life itself, including the challenges that it brings us.
- Love yourself—you are then free to love everyone.
- When you stop loving yourself, loneliness results.
- Love the substance not the form. Look beyond the outer shell.
- You love everyone—that's the choice.
- Have absolute confidence in the power of love.
- If you want to be loved, then love.

Loving Life

Love as input fills the heart

Awake and present, play your part

Live in love, now and gain

Or live in the past, attached with pain

Deluded, angered – ignorant acts

Love and wise – the good facts

Love it is the master seed,

Nourished generate many good deed

Magic jars – wisdom and love

Work together – hand in glove

Give away love, end up with more

Restrict your love, shrink your core

Give the wisdom, more it grows

To a life that's full, more it flows

Love's not a virtue, but is a need

Important as water and the food to feed

You cannot hoard, but only give

Enables a life – you truly live

If Love Appears to Be Missing

If you come across a humangee who appears to be missing love, consider the following:

Observing complaints, consider what it was like to live in a world where spurious complaining was deemed appropriate.

Observing insults, understand that this person learned early that it's okay to abuse others.

Observing anger, see the pain of isolation and the insecurity or lack of love from others.

Observing disconnection, think about what causes it, and ask if your response will widen the gulf between the two of you.

Observing extremism or fundamentalism, see the vacuum and need for belonging and desire to provide a solution to the empytness if they risked letting go.

Observing controlling behavior, understand the duality and separation that must have bred it.

Observing always needing to be right, appreciate how often this humangee was made to be, sense, and feel wrong.

Observing passive-aggressiveness, recognize the child that wasn't taught a safe way to express their opinion or love.

Observing obnoxiousness, recognize that bravado or arrogance belies the soul that has been led to believe that "I'm not enough."

Observing selfishness, wonder what it might be like to walk the world with a feeling of lack, insecurity, and depletion.

Observing drama or attention-seeking, see the person who wishes so much to be seen and to be acknowledged or needed.

Observing accusation, imagine what it might be like to live through a life filled with suspicion.

Observing judgment or comparisons, step into the opportunity the world has just provided you for practicing love and acceptance.

Observing criticism, consider and imagine what it might have been like to be raised to see only what is wrong.

Observing fierce hatred, believe in the possibility that there exists the potential for equally intense, beautiful loyalty and love.

Observing any of the above, realize the need for compassion and the understanding of what has led to this point. When we come to our time to die, it is not the size of our house or bank balance that will give us satisfaction, but whether we lived an authentic life full of love.

Help me please

We doubt our lovability, so we crave to be loved by others. But the falser we are to ourselves, the less we love ourselves. The less we love ourselves, the more we crave to be loved by others.

We do anything for attention. We will play victim and do whatever it takes just to be noticed.

When you realize what and who you are, it is easy to love yourself.

—Inspired by the teachings of Shane Mulhall

Love and Desire

We made a clear distinction between love that is limited or restricted and that which is unlimited. Where love is limited, duality exists: we see ourselves as different or other, unlike someone else. This is compounded by conventional conditioning, where we're taught to strive for successes, attainments, and validation of various kinds. And while achieving a level of success is laudable, we need to be wary of the intent and emotion behind it.

Can you find in yourself a love for yourself and for others? Or is there selfishness, disregard, disrespect, thoughtlessness, or even disdain for others?

A better appreciation of the full concept of desire can help us discern between wholesome and unwholesome desire. Desire we might find is a truly unhealthy Trojan horse into the mind of humangee.

Chapter 15

Want: Desires and Ego

Trapped by Desire

Many years ago, while humangee were still evolving, there were two neighboring tribes of primitive humangee.

One tribe was called the Innies, as they were internally focused. And the other tribe was called the Outies, since they were outwardly focused.

The two tribes were noticeably different. The Innies just wanted to have fun, were a bit child-like, and were quite relaxed. They took time each day to be still, and apparently paused between events. They were known to have high attention to detail when they were focused and when they worked or were perfecting their craft. They seemed to work less than the Outies and had a good balance between work and play. They didn't take themselves too seriously and worked together with others in the tribe for common goals.

The Outies were well organized and worked hard to improve themselves. They had a very good work ethic and were focused on achieving their goals. They were always keen to make their tribe suc-cessful and were very competitive. They took themselves and others seriously but were also in favor of a good party. They were natural multitaskers but sometimes got bored with things or didn't enjoy their lives as much as they would like. They were generally always aiming to improve. They liked to venture into other areas and

to get nice things. They also seemed to be a bit more stressed, intense, or aggressive than the Innies.

Each tribe thought it was smarter than the other.

The two tribes knew each other and for the most part relationships were good.

However, occasionally the Innies had a favorite joke that they would play on the Outies. They would prove they were smarter; look how dumb the Outies were.

The Innies used to put some of their favorite fragrant foods in a narrow-necked jar, which was then buried sufficiently in the ground somewhere in between the two tribes villages. Outies could smell the food and locate it to the hole in the ground. At this stage, the primitive humangee was already excited. When it reached into the narrow but shallow hole in the ground, they could touch it, feel it, smell it, and almost taste it. Oooh yeah!

It was a big piece, so it took their whole hand to hold it. But when they tried to take it out of the hole, it was stuck. The combination of the food and their hand was too big to get it back out through the hole. They would try and try, but would not let go of the food, lest they lose it. Hence, they could not get the food out, and they could not escape. They would squeal in their efforts to get it out or to get away.

Then as the Innies moved in slowly, laughing and giggling, to capture, tickle, or help them, the Outies would squeal even more, because they were trapped.

The Innies innately knew of the problem with many desires and attachments. That once a mental attachment is made it is very hard, and often impossible, to let go of. And for those with an outward focus, it's an easy trap.

They understood that the key requirement is to let go and, immediately, freedom is returned.

Apparently, the game still goes on to this day. And it never ceases to produce the same pleasure for the Innies and frustration for the Outies.

This reinforces the Innies' view of Outies' lack of insight or intelligence—not only do they continually get trapped by the ploy, but they never seem to learn!

Ego, Attachment, Wants, and Desires

We are born to live, breathe, play, work, eat, and enjoy life in the physical active world. We are also designed to live free, content, blissful lives in the mental world. However, most humangee spend practically all of their time in the former and none in the latter. That is, most spend little time truly in the present moment and in the still, quiet inner world.

One of the consequences is that we come to believe that the physical world is the only one that exists or matters (sometimes called "the illusion").

As a consequence, the typical humangee concentrates on satisfying the needs and wants of the transient day-to-day physical world.

The basic desires and needs for food, shelter, security, and company were outlined in the hierarchy of needs in chapter 3. As the lower ones are met, humangee have a choice to focus on the higher-level awakening aspects or on physical world desires.

These desires are "wants" rather than needs. Some desires are necessary; this is acceptable in balance, and it is very helpful if humangee is awake to the distinction. Hence our use of the word desire in this chapter and throughout this manual relates to these personal, selfish wants.

The key aspect here is to understand and appreciate the ego; realize that, like a bad habit, it feeds on "want-desires." These desires, if unmanaged, enlarge and expand the ego. This is one of the key mind components that we discussed in chapter 6. It is a fundamental aspect of mind, as shown on the mind model set out below. Ego and desire go hand in hand.

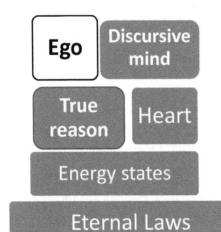

Ego and desires are an aspect of our mind that we need to manage

Are Desires the Eternal Enemy of Humangee?

According to the Bhagavad Gita, the Hindu scripture, desires are the constant enemy of the wise. When we think of objects, we form an attachment to them. From attachment grows longing, and from longing grows anger. From anger comes delusion, and from delusion comes loss of memory. From loss of memory, one loses discrimination. Then from ruin of discrimination, humangee perishes.

Again, we may view the jump from one assertion to the next in the statement above as being tenuous, but it is worth considering relevant examples in your own life.

We also know that all master teachers advocate freedom from desires.

Desireless Utopia

If most humangee were offered a desireless life, few would take it. It doesn't sound attractive. It doesn't sound like something

that would make us happy. In fact, we believe the opposite, that it would make us less happy than we are now. It sounds like a non-life, without vision, aspirations, or real joy. This lack of appreciation or understanding of the desireless life causes real problems.

With regard to desire, humangee normally experience three states:

- **Normal waking state:** full of activity, agitation, movement, and desire.
- **Dreaming state:** where the mind plays with the impressions of unfulfilled desires.
- **Sleeping state:** in deep sleep humangee is desireless and perfectly content. There is a level of freedom, contentment, and bliss.

There is a fourth state: True waking state. This offers limitless rest, peace, and joy, beyond deep sleep.

However, as long as desires exist, this state cannot be attained. Hence desire is the blocker to this fourth state of true rest, true joy, and true peace.

> *Desire enters the house of man as a guest and soon becomes a host. He finally ends up as the master, where the man is reduced to a servant.*
>
> *The freeman is enslaved by his own desires.*
>
> —Shane Mulhall

Despite the truthfulness and simplicity of this principle or argument, virtually every person dedicates themselves to the fulfillment of desires.

So how can such a simple but big mistake occur?

We'll call it the Trojan horse of desire. It goes like this:

A humangee called Mac is desireless and perfectly happy. Mac sees a friend, Sam, who has got a new car, which looks nice. Sam looks very happy. A desire arises in Mac, and with that comes a level of discontentment. Consequently, an urge arises to work toward getting a nice car, and Mac takes action to earn extra money to make that happen. Mac buys a new car and is satisfied.

However, a big mistake is made. Mac believes that the attainment of the goal and the new car and the associated kudos has brought the happiness. And while there may be some truth in that, the key contributor to the new happiness was the return to the desireless state.

Happiness does not come from the attainment of the object, but from the removal of the desire—and hence the return of the desireless state.

We do not have to attain objects to be free from desire. We can simply drop the desire and save all the striving.

We all have experience of the latter, dropping of a desire. For example, we could be focused on doing something as part of a plan, and a friend stops by or something of interest distracts us, and we go with it. Before you know it fifteen minutes has passed and the desire has been forgotten, at least temporarily.

With desirelessness, we have contentment, with no agitation or striving. We achieve rest, which is what humangee ultimately wants, but desires will not let us rest.

Conversely, one gets continuous happiness with desirelessness. Happiness does not arise from any external object. It comes from within.

Becoming a Beggar or a Trader

When one develops an attraction for another thing, person, creature, object, there is an assumption that this will make me happy. A chase or activity takes place to get the thing and thus a happiness external to myself is required. Humangee is turned into a beggar, hoper, pray-er, pleading for more, desiring health, fitness, wealth, power, house, car, freedom from troubles, the basic necessities of life. Humangee becomes a trader, because he/she sells themselves for objects in return.

Humangee trade our health, accumulating wealth. We then trade our wealth trying to restore our health.

Humangee will even trade love. *I will love you if you love me. I will continue to love you if you make me happy.*

There is no end to the desires to fill the heart—from a child and toys, to teenager, to youth, to young adult, to mature adult. Feeding the desires does not make them go away, they simply grow in strength and number. Desires are the fuel of the ego.

Feeding desires is like putting coal on a fire in the hope that it will put it out. It will not.

How or why do desires arise? Humangee's natural state is awake, insightful, and happy.

However, when we identify with body and mind, we come to believe that we are limited. Even so, deep down in memory, we know we are complete.

Humangee is confused by the limits of the body and the mind and thus desires to expand, to rid oneself of these limits by acquisition of these objects.

In deep sleep there is no identification with the body and mind nor any knowledge of work, play, home, challenges, family, or activities. There is no desire.

The outcome of desire is misery. Strange as it may seem, all desires come from identifying with the body and mind, particularly when it is not awake or present.

Happiness arises in desirelessness, but it gets covered in desire. This is the fundamental mistake. This causes humangee to follow their desire and come to believe that happiness is external to the self.

Here is the crux:

If we do not come to see and recognize this to be true, then we will never be free from desire.

The consequence of this is that we will never be truly happy.

(Yep, you read that right.)

What Are Desires?

They are simply our eternal search to enjoy our true nature: truth, consciousness, and bliss, wisdom, awareness, and contentment.

Like their nature, they want their desires fulfilled totally and permanently. Nobody wants to be temporarily happy.

But a humangee can only desire according to his or her knowledge.

Hence this varies by age and the accompanying wants at that stage. A four-year-old wants toys, a fourteen-year-old wants a mobile phone, a sixty-year-old wants a holiday in the sun, and so on.

- If the knowledge is limited or false, then the desire is under ignorance.
- If the desire is under ignorance, then the fruit of that desire is under ignorance.
- Under ignorance, desire is the food of the ego. And that's what keeps it alive.

- With ego comes further desire under ignorance.

Effect of desire on the body under ignorance:

With respect to physical action, when desire is in the humangee, energy pours out of the body. Like the first time you learn to drive, the first time you walk across a stage, the first time you speak in public. Anytime you're trying too hard or doing something you are uncomfortable with, you are exhausted afterward.

Ease in the body is replaced by disease. The body carries tension. When there is a high level of desire and thus self-induced tension to perform an action, our nervous system activates a response mechanism.

Effects of desire on the mind under ignorance:

1. You're frequently changing your mind.

2. Jobs are started and not finished, and you move on to something else.

3. You are unable to focus for very long. Driving, studying, giving attention to a task, listening. Desire splits the mind between past and future.

4. Your desire overcomes your knowledge. We inherently know what is right and wrong in an action, but we choose to ignore the signals. We think that we can get away with it. We mistake pleasure for happiness.
   - We suffer from the revolving wheel of pleasure and pain.
   - We know what to do, but we choose not to do it.

- We ignore the consequences.
  - We overeat, and ignore the consequences of becoming fat.
  - We undereat, and ignore the consequences of doing harm to our body.
  - We overwork, and ignore the consequences to our relationships.

5. We lie to ourselves. We deceive ourselves with optimistic justifications. For example, I can leave late and still get there on time. I can tell a small lie and no one will know.

6. Loss of intelligence or capability.

Effects of desire on the heart:

1. It contracts the heart.

When one shifts from love to attachments or desire, there is no or little concern for other people's needs.

2. It results in impure emotions, including dissatisfaction and unbridled ambition. Under ignorance, the mind is never happy with what it has and is always looking for something quite different.

While the poor humangee envies the comforts of the rich and wants to be rich too, the rich humangee is weary from anxieties and envies the carefree life of the one who has nothing and no worries. A sick woman worries about getting well while a woman in good health worries about getting sick.

Humangee get a fancy to something and are willing to go to any length to get it. They commit to it, and it occupies body, mind, heart, and will. They are willing to sacrifice their possessions and relationships to get it. With desire in the heart, there comes a growth of impatience, anger, and hatred.

One becomes impatient if one's desires are delayed.

One becomes angry if one's desires are obstructed.

One learns to hate if one's desires are prevented.

All anger is desire frustrated. It has no other source. The deeper the desire the greater the hate when it is frustrated.

3. Relationships are impaired or destroyed.

Love is the natural magnetism in any relationship. And when it is so, there is harmony, unity, and peace.

But when there is desire and difference between two parties, there is friction, anger, envy, and meanness of heart.

If this arises between two people and becomes excessive, it can lead to controlling and manipulation of one's spouse, child, property, wealth, boyfriend, girlfriend, or partner.

Desire in the heart brings an increase in suffering. Consider two such cases:

a. Desire leads to exaggerated expectation of the final outcome.

Take exams, for example. One student is happy on finishing senior exams, but as soon as she has the results in hand, they don't satisfy her expectations. This applies to many other areas of the unawakened humangee life. The expectation of achieving the desire often results in an anticlimax or disappointment. And thus, a desire for something else arises.

b. Increase in grief or sorrow.

It's a harsh law that if you desire things that die then you will surely grieve. There is no escape from this truth. Those who are awake approach death and grief from a different perspective.

Desire under Knowledge

Humangee are designed to enjoy truth, consciousness, and bliss.

But having forgotten their nature, they form three desires:

1. To live forever
2. To know everything
3. To be happy always

This evolves to a natural longing or desire for a finer and brighter life, to bring humangee closer to unity.

> Desires which evolve to the acquisition of truth, knowledge, and bliss are not the ones that are the enemy of humangee.

How do we eliminate desire under ignorance while allowing for growth in desire under knowledge?

If desires are fulfilled indiscriminately, then desire arises again. If they are suppressed, then anger and resentment can arise to confuse the mind. The third way is to reduce false desires and grow true ones in humangee. Consider the following directions:

1. Practice discrimination. Determine that the acquisition of excessive worldly things will not bring happiness. Review all habitual desires and drop those that are not conducive to happiness and freedom.

After a desire arises, there is always an innate natural prompt to ask whether it is right or wrong or good or bad. This may be very subtle or hardly noticeable. But because we are commonly in a hurry, desire propels us. Generally, we don't listen and respond. We just react under habit.

Similar to the opportunity after an event or stimulus, there is a micro-second in which we can choose to react or pause and respond. There is a silent knowledge that arises between the desire arising and the action being initiated. Practice observing this pause; be present and awake.

2. Read what the sages have said. Or go to someone who knows or attend an appropriate school. Use knowledge that has passed the test of time and practical validation. Evaluate and pursue self-inquiry.

3. Practice detachment. Witness the events of life: using the play analogy (from chapter 4) not just of your own life and events, but those of others around you. It could be as simple as being in a sales showroom where there is a buyer, seller, and an observer, or some other environment. The observer has no bias or attachment.

4. Practice letting go. We have to learn to release our hold on the events of life, which we store unconsciously. This includes forgiving. When we see ourselves becoming attached, we must let go.

5. Give up the attachment to the results. Thou hast the right to work, but not to the fruits thereof. Surrender to the activity, respond to the need alone, and move on!

Notice with a great judge or surgeon how nothing is attached or carried forward, and skill is not impaired if a bad event occurs. Focus on the process as you do not control the outcome.

In addition, embrace the following practices that help dissolve desires under ignorance and promote desires under knowledge:

a. Serve others. Fulfilling one's duties to others, rather than claiming one's own rights, purifies the heart.

One's own desires are starved and diminish.

This, together with purification, frees one from desire.

b. Meditate. This practice brings the mind to stillness. This is helpful both during and after the practice. That means that the effects of the meditation continue into the periods between meditation sessions.

A still mind finds happiness in everything. Additionally, it brings you to a place of deep bliss, where the craving for lesser pleasures falls away.

c. Enlarge the interval between desires. Between each desire is a natural interval and an opportunity to come to rest. But we generally don't take the rest.

If asked how our day was, we can recite the activities, but rarely focus on the rest in between. Maybe that's because we didn't take it or didn't want to be seen to be taking it.

Allow yourself the luxury of a little rest between events, and ultimately enlarge it up to five minutes. Like the wood-cutter sharpening the saw, it makes for more effective work in the same or less time.

d. Enjoy good company. Good material, content, people, and a group of like-minded thinkers. That which contributes to the presence of good thoughts and feelings in the mind and heart. This is covered in more detail in chapter 16.

e. Promote the desire for liberation or freedom. This form of desire can be used as a mechanism to align any other desires in one direction; aligned desire is freedom. We must understand what true freedom is, and that we have a choice in how and when we give it away. When faced with a desire or decision, we can ask the question: Is this action conducive to my freedom? And then act accordingly.

Everyone is free but thinks that they are bound.

Consider the story at the start of the chapter about being trapped by desire.

Be careful what you attach to, because the moment you are bound to something, the contentment will disappear.

Give attention to the action and not the outcome.

Before undertaking any action, an ordinary worldly humangee always tries to assess what benefit they will accrue as a result. But a realized or awake humangee undertakes it as a matter of duty, with no desire for its consequent benefits.

A correct attitude makes real wealth. One who possesses this wealth is never poor.

With regard to your house, car, clothing, and assets, it's fine to enjoy them for living, but you should not consider them as belonging to you.

Consider instead that these items are the property of the universe. They are gifts on loan to you. And if you look after them well, then that is good.

Chains of desire

The same goes for the gift of children. We do not own them. We are custodians for a period, and our opportunity is to enjoy the gift and provide good stewardship.

Our desires are like strings that pull us toward the world. We choose how many strings are added and how hard they are pulled.

If we remember that our body, mind, and heart are a gift over which we have stewardship, any actions, including eating, drinking, working, relaxation, enjoyment, and looking after our humangee, are with respect that it is on loan from the universe. (See Software License Agreement in Appendix 3)

Filters and Pop-up Blockers

The mind is constantly throwing up thoughts for consideration. And most unawake people assume they have to follow these thoughts. This is not the case.

They are like ads that come up on your TV, PC, phone, or social media site. As a device user, you will know to avoid the ad or skim it and move on. Only if it is particularly relevant to you at that moment in time will you even consider clicking or following the ad. If you are tech savvy, you will apply a pop-up blocker or be careful on your privacy settings. You may even pay for a premium version of the service, just to stop these unwanted interruptions in your attention and focus. The fact is that you exercise at least some sense of control over them.

Humangee just let the thought-ads bombard us all day, every day; we think that is normal. It is not. If only you could have the same level of clinical discernment to the thoughts that are served to your humangee device-mind as you do to your phone. You would exercise freedom from these fleeting ideas as they come into your mind.

❚❚

Well, the good news is you can. But you need to invest the time and effort into reducing the old habit. Most of us are thought-ad junkies and we don't realize it. We are simply asleep to the constant flow of these thought-ads that come into our mind on a daily basis.

A key starting point is to be more awake to observe these thoughts coming in, realize what they are, and understand that they do not need our attention.

This could mean thinking about work when you're at home. It could mean worries that float into your awareness at unlikely moments, or it could be an irritating event from a few days ago that you're ruminating on. It could be literally anything. Most people do not apply a filter to these thoughts; they have no idea how they can.

This is where the pause, mindfulness, and meditation practices come in. This is how we build the rewiring to be alert to these old habits.

The thought balloons on the cartoon below are made in the discursive mind (see chapter 6). Rather than latching on to them and giving them life, we can use our own pop-up blocker, like a pin to the balloon. Or we can simply ignore the thought and let it drift away.

The key is one of minimal effort: just forget about them and revert to the present activity. Give your focus over to the task at hand.

**When thoughts arise,
we can pop them or just let go**

❚❚ ▶ ■

The Pimple of Desire

A twenty something humangee called Meg has a pimple on her face. To her this is no ordinary pimple—it is obvious, bold, and proud as a beacon. In truth, it is quite small. Our humangee has an aversion for the pimple and it seeks to find a way to get rid of it. So, she goes online and searches for a solution. She spends some time researching these pimples and even watches a few YouTube videos. In short, she gains some revealing insight into the murky pimple world, after which she chooses to buy some magic pimple cream. She clicks BUY and goes on with her week, waiting in anticipation. The big day comes, a small parcel containing the cream arrives. She reads both the box and the instructions, like any good patient would, and notices a comment, "It might work, it might not." No comment.

She opens the tube and puts the cream on the offending miniature volcano-pimple and then crosses her fingers.

When she gets up the next morning, lo and behold, just like magic, the pimple is gone. Excitement emerges. She is pleased and proud that it is gone and that she can now go out in public again. Life is good and normalcy has been restored.

The next morning when she gets up, she has a good stretch and goes into the bathroom. When she glances in the mirror, she is taken aback. There are now two pimples looking at her. Initially she is disappointed, but that soon fades as she knows that she has the cream and can put it on them. The cream works well and by night time the two pimples have subsided and are practically invisible.

The following morning, when she goes to the bathroom, she is shocked to see that there are now four pimples. How can this be? A bit deflated, she puts on the cream and is a bit less enthusiastic for her day and is a tad subdued. That evening the four pimples have settled a bit, but not as much as before.

She wakens early the next morning, doesn't bother stretching, and goes straight to the bathroom. She is horrified to see she now has eight pimples, like a small mountain range. After the shock, she is bewildered and confused. *What should I do? What can I do?*

She decides to use the cream since it had some good reviews, and people had mentioned that it can take a few days for the pimples to go away. But she decides to make an appointment with the doctor. Just in case. But she can't get an appointment for three days.

She chooses not to go outside and spends time inside doing more pimple research and watching old shows. The next day, when she goes into the bathroom, her worst fears have been realized—she now has sixteen pimples. Things are not good. A level of sadness ensues, and the time disappears in a dream state until her appointment with the doctor.

She goes to the clinic, brings the cream with her, and explains to the doctor what has happened. The doctor listens attentively and asks a few other questions. Then she says to Meg, "The cream causes the pimple. Stop using it. Get rid of it. The other things that you are doing are just fine. If you continue to look after your body well and eat clean, natural foods, they will go away."

And they did.

Cream causes pimple

Some addictions and habits are like the cream. If you are a smoker, a chocaholic, a drinker, or a substance user, it's worth realizing that, to your mind, use reinforces use, cream causes pimple.

Take potato chips, sweets, or fizzy drinks as an example. If we have a desire for these substances, consuming them does not make the desire go away. It feeds the desire and habit. It is putting coal on the desire-fire. It's cream on the pimple. A state of desirelessness has not been achieved. Realize that if you don't use the cream, the pimples will go away by themselves. Make the decision not to feed your desires. Don't use the cream.

Seeing the Substance versus the Form

In the physical external world, we generally tend to see the form and not consider the substance. We see the outside façade or surface and not necessarily the inside.

Simple examples of substance and form include gold and ring, clay and pot, plastic and ruler. The latter is simply a temporary, visible presentation of the former.

In terms of humangee, most see the outer body, mind, and form but not the inner essence and heart. It is helpful to see this distinction for all objects whether natural or man-made.

In the case of humangee, seeing the substance dissolves the illusion and allows you to see behind the form to the essence. Higher reason reveals the substance.

It is worth considering that if something has no true substance, it cannot satisfy! If one focuses only on form, this is transient and is insufficient to fully satisfy the heart.

Take "husband" and "wife," for example. These are just roles or forms. There is something behind these forms. Imagine the husband and wife have a disagreement or irritation. Their tendency may be to focus purely on the event, the current presenting problem, rather than the essence. The focus is on the difference and not the unity. If we can start from the acknowledgment of substance, from the position of unity, there is a good chance that the source of irritation can be properly articulated, understood, and addressed.

For humangee, the substance is the essence of the being (see chapter 3). The substance is permanent, the form is transient. Unawake humangee continually miss the substance and value only the form—in whatever guise it takes that day.

The analogy of gold and ring is physical. Consider the following more subtle mind distinctions for **substance and form**:

- Silence & sound
- Stillness & activity
- Unmoving & moving
- Permanent & transient
- Source & manifestation
- Universe & Earth
- Essence & humangee

» For example, stillness and silence are always there. If you really want to hear the sound, you have to hear the silence. All sound takes place against silence.
» Similarly, all action takes place against the backdrop of stillness.
» All movement and activity take place against the backdrop of the unmoving.

Iceberg—Substance

From a different perspective, we could use the example below. Often, all of what we see is the superficial. When we look closer and experience a bit deeper, we can see there is something beyond the surface veneer. There is often something more substantial and foundational. There is a substance to the iceberg's form.

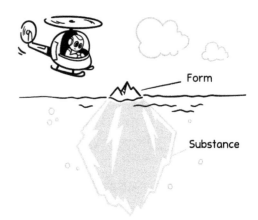

Being present and seeing the substance beyond the forms and events apparent to us each day is supported by the faculty of reason, which is the subject of our next chapter.

Chapter 16
True Reason

This is reason under truth as opposed to reason under ignorance—an important distinction.

What Is True Reason? (Reason)

It is a natural power of the mind.

It is available in the state of awakeness, stillness, and clarity. It reveals truth from untruth, right from wrong, large from small, outer from inner, substance from form.

It is a natural capability for our use. Hence lives should be lived in accordance with reason and our true nature.

It holds perfection in the mind and measures against that perfection. It gives the power of discrimination or discernment to the human being. And with this, humangee enjoys choice and, thus, has free will.

Without the faculty of true reason, the life progresses full of doubt and error.

In the light of true reason, quality of action is improved, and work is completed with efficiency and attention. At the highest level, it shows unity. It unifies everything, exhibiting peace and harmony.

It is one of the four primary components of our operating system model.

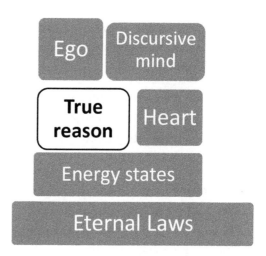

Reason is to the mind what love is to the heart. Both are facilities of the essence or soul. They are tools for humangee use, to enable a naturally balanced life.

True Reason Is Essential for Humangee

Love and reason are natural to the human being, but they need to be awakened.

And then like any good habit or discipline, they need to be stabilized and naturalized (i.e., to become habitual).

It is as natural, easy, and effortless for the human being to reason as it is to walk. We have the capacity to reason, but not all use it!

Since it is already there and is natural, all efforts with regard to reason are to remove blockages to being reasonable. That is, simply to allow it to operate.

Reason Is Enjoyable

We all want to be reasonable; we are happy in reason. No humangee wants to be seen as unreasonable. If someone is accused of being unreasonable, they will stop or object. Unawake humangee want or need to justify being unreasonable.

Reason is like the orangeness of an orange. You can't take it out. You can never lose reason. It is always with you. You may not use it, but you never lose it.

What is reason?

- What stands to reason is true.
- Reason liberates and reveals the truth.
- Reason gives you certainty.
- Higher reason dissolves the illusion.

In chapter 6 we showed that reason is one of the key components of our mind, working along with other parts to enable us to function the way we do.

It is the component that assimilates information and enables us to reach conclusions, to provide recommendations in making decisions.

So, if there is no reason in the humangee, the body will always pursue pleasure and avoid pain. It has no choice about it! It's the way it works. If one wants a conscious, awake life, then reason is essential.

Reason versus Reasoning

In this context, reason or reasoning is not the analytical thinking through of a problem or challenge unless the mind is still and peaceful. It operates best when insight or information has been gathered, the mind is still and clear, and true reason is allowed to operate.

True reason operates

Reason is unable to operate

Reason in your mind and love in your heart allows humangee to align to true nature

It is natural to be reasonable.

What Causes Lack of Reason in Humangee?

Many things can cause lack of reason; a few are discussed below. All fit into the category of false or erroneous ideas and beliefs.

1. False ideas

Having false ideas about all kinds of things causes us to be unreasonable. Ideas about anger, happiness, work, family, friends, relationships, and love.

For example, we might have been told in childhood that it is not good to suppress anger. So, we vent it. We believe the recommendation to be true. But it's not true; it's not reasonable. These are the same as the misconceptions or misunderstandings discussed in chapter 10.

We might have false ideas about happiness and think things outside of us can make us happy or unhappy, like traffic jams or missing a bus or the train coming early. This misery is self-created.

2. False beliefs

The same is true for false beliefs. For example, if I believe that I can be very selfish and it won't have negative consequences, I'm blocked from true reason. Another false belief is the consideration that freedom is being able to do whatever I want to do. It is impossible to do this, as one person's freedom often affects others. Wise law liberates and facilitates freedom. False beliefs result in lack of reason.

3. Fixed or limited perceptions and seeking what may seem right only within a small context

For example, humangee often seek to exercise their rights. This could be in work or in relation to government. But this is often done without due regard for both rights and duties of all. Duties should come first. One might observe that few aggressively claim their duties. With true reason, you can't demand your rights before you fulfill your duties. Ideally, the wider context of any event or situation should be observed in order for true reason to be seen in operation.

4. Erroneous idea of rest

This causes an ill-measured life and denies how the creation works. When one looks objectively at the physical creation, everything decays—the law of entropy applies. Hence within this physical aspect of our world there is essentially no rest. Things are always subject to change. A mind that is active or agitated is not at rest.

However, there is rest in stillness.

One needs to step inside, to the realm of stillness. There one will find rest.

5. Erroneous ideas about our happiness

Some people believe that things make them sad, angry, frustrated, or happy. But we now know that this is a choice. When one is in a waking-dream state (unawake), all misery is self-created.

If we believe we are dependent on things, then typically we are afraid of losing them. Consequently, we feel the need to control them. And with control comes a form of imprisonment and demand.

External things or events do not have the capacity to make humangee sad. Only the interpretations we put on them.

What blocks access to reason?

1. Desires

Natural desires that are common to all, like food, drink, money to live are fine in measure. Other desires that are personal or special to me or any other humangee cause one to be unreasonable. The key here is that reason is overturned or trumped by desire.

Access to reason can be blocked when people are fixated on any strong preference (e.g., my car parking space; my space on the road; expectations placed on me at work or by a friend; my attachments to a sports team, an outcome, or competition). This often generates strong reactions and has scope to override an awake response.

Humangee has capacity to manufacture justifications.

With desire active in our being, we may disregard what we know to be true.

The desire or mental habit essentially dislodges the use of reason. Both common sense and reason are often overcome by desire.

We succumb to desires every day, knowing that there is a better alternative, believing that it won't do much harm.

When reason is forgotten?

2. Ideas or "values"

Ideas like it's a sad day, he is a nasty person, this is a depressing event, that's a great result, this is miserable rain are all a form of labelling. This personal pigeonholing or perception actually reflects more about us, the holder, than the reality itself. We think that the values or assessments are true, but they rarely are. Or they're certainly not the full story.

The same event can be experienced two totally different ways. For someone who has decided that they don't like rain, they see "miserable rain."

People experience events, other people, and aspects of life differently. To a farmer in the third week of a drought, the rain could be wonderful. But the next day when going on holiday, it is terrible.

Reason reveals the true value of everything. It is happy and never fooled. If these values or ideas are untrue, it is unreasonable.

If we see unreasonable valuation of something by someone else, like an excessive reaction, we observe it to be unreasonable. We are blind to our own unreasonable valuations.

3. Lack of willpower also blocks reason

With reason, you have immediate illumination.

Lack of willpower and discipline cause us to be unreasonable.

Our values are not constant. But we always believe that they are true at the time.

Reason and decision-making

While reason enables absolute clarity to see a solution all at once, it doesn't do anything.

You have to make a choice. You can reject the recommendation. Will you accept or reject what reason has conveyed?

When does reason operate? We overviewed the three main states of mind in Energy States in chapter 6. Reason operates in the state of stillness or clarity. See the following summary:

- **Stillness (Awake):** Mind is clear, lucid, bright, perceptive. Decisions do not change.
- **Frenetic or Active:** Reason will not operate: doubt, lack of certainty. Mind changes with the mood, rushed, receive new data. It's a frantic approach to making a decision and can result in poorly thought through actions or deferral to get more information or insight that may or may not be of any true further help.
- **Dull or Relaxed:** The state is apathy, tired, uninspired, without conviction, fixed or rigid. Fixity is a way to be unreasonable. There can be certainty, which can be completely wrong. Hence, we can be convinced but have the wrong convictions.

Desires, Habits, and Reactions

Habits are … habitual. Like puppets, we just do them automatically. We are on automatic pilot. There is no application check box like on your device app to ask: Are you sure you want to proceed Y/N?

In this state, true reason is not fully operational.

There are many reasons why and how these routines develop. At this stage in this manual, it is sufficient to say that the being is not fully present when the habit stimulus and associated reaction occurs. It could be to eat, worry, smoke, react to something in a preprogrammed way or something else. If it's a well-established habit, most human-gee will have low confidence that they can

consistently override the stimulus without succumbing.

So, the starting point is to be awake and observe the stimulus event. Be present at this time. Pause and observe whether it is supporting your well-being before you respond. The response is a choice, not a reaction.

There is a short window of time between the stimulus and the reaction or response. The key is to spot the stimulus event and realize that you have the opportunity to be awake and start to break the habit reaction. When you do this consistently, you can then decide how you choose to address it going forward. So, the starting point is to be awake to the event or habit and come into the present. Dissolution of the habit can progress from here, when this level of awareness has been raised.

Between stimulus and response, there is a fraction of a second (or a window of opportunity/ time) to pause and to choose your response rather than react out of habit or pre-programming. And even if you don't change the habit immediately, spotting the gap consistently is a good start.

When you spot it you got it

How do we awaken our reason?

You may start to see some familiar recommendations arising from here on. If so, that is good, because the practices are consistent, and they build on each other across all areas of life.

First, keep "good company." This is a collective term to convey that which feeds our mind and heart. These inputs should be of a good and suitable nature. Hence it refers to more than just the people we choose to associate with. Whenever possible, find others with an open mind who are on a similar journey to discover the best in themselves and others.

Good company can include good reading, audio, or video material. As usual, examine this content to test the assumptions to ensure they are based on truth. In the same way that there is fake news, consider that there is fake advice and fake wisdom. One needs to validate these either in practice or with a teacher or trustworthy source. This can include study of the words of the wise or scripture. Any facilitator of this personal awakening should be a committed inquirer into wisdom and truth, one who practices appropriate self-analysis and honesty. Not all purveyors of wisdom and truth have the same critical and discerning mind as Plato. So, seek advice from the best. The net effect is these inputs support purity and refinement of feelings and thoughts in our heart and mind.

Growing Reason and Resolve

Reason has to be awakened in us and grows stronger with practice and refinement.

In the same way we wash the body to avoid it being dirty over time, we need to wash the mind and heart. This is achieved through regular pausing, falling still, mindful activity, and proper meditation.

Developing reason takes time, so resolve to stay the course.

Cumulative Effect

We may now understand a bit more about the importance of being present, about how love, heart, happiness, service, reason, and responsibility come together. And we might have some insight into attachments, aversions, desires, and other thoughts or habits that may move us in the wrong direction.

In the next chapter, we'll examine how these aspects operate together.

Reason and Wisdom

The farmer's truck

There was once a wise humangee farmer who lived on a small farm on the outskirts of town. He lived a modest life with his wife and their daughter. One day, for no apparent reason, a fine pickup truck was left at his farm. There was no identification; the driver left no message. It was brand new and had the keys and owner's book inside. The farmer and his wife asked in the town and called the vehicle licensing office to find out who owned it. There was no record, but it was paid for. So they were allowed to keep it.

When their friends saw them, they said how fortunate they were. The farmer replied, maybe we are, maybe we're not.

They put the truck to good work and kept it nice and clean.

Several months later, however, the truck was stolen.

A week went by, then two weeks, and they were losing hope that they would get it back. Their friends said how unfortunate they were to have their prized possession taken from them. The farmer said, maybe we are, maybe we aren't.

The following month, the truck was found (and the people who had taken it were caught), and there was some money in it. The police checked with the thieves, who said they had no idea where it came from. So, the police said to the farmer that, since it was his truck, it was now his money. Some of their friends got to hear of this and said how lucky they were. The farmer responded saying, maybe we are, maybe we are not.

Months passed, and the daughter was driving the truck (faster than she would drive her own car), and a deer jumped out onto the road. She veered to miss it and hit a tree and was quite badly hurt. She was rushed to hospital. When the farmer and his wife were talking to friends later, they said how unfortunate, it was a tragic event, and that the truck was cursed, and they were so unlucky. To which the farmer responded, maybe it is, maybe it isn't.

However, when the daughter was in the hospital, they were able to fix a pre-existing hip condition that had been a problem for years. She previously had a bad limp, but now, when she came out of hospital, her hip and leg were perfect, and

she could walk elegantly and was very happy.

Days after, the friends saw the family and said how lucky they were and that the truck was blessed. The farmer said, maybe it is, maybe it isn't.

They still have the truck today. ☺

As the story illustrates, one cannot appreciate or judge an event or events, a person or people in isolation.

**Over time:
Maybe it is, maybe it isn't**

Chapter 17
A Direction for Life

The key objective for the manual and for humangee life is to wake up to reality, to the helicopter view of life. To see your life from a distance rather than the dream state life when down walking in the depths of the forest.

From this position of observation, the world is seen in a different and good way. You see the day-to-day aspects with much more objective clarity than you would otherwise.

The Challenge and Opportunity of a Fully Congruent Life

The following section is intended to make us ask the hard questions of ourselves and ultimately to think and reflect on our lives.

The first part is a blunt and direct observation of many dream state lives. It is intended to provoke self-inquiry and finishes with recommendations that align with the other conclusions in the manual.

Our True Capacity versus What Manifests

We know we have greater capacity than we are currently using. Most humangee do not discover how to live until it's time to die. However, they die to themselves at a very early age and are only buried at the expiration of the body, decades later.

The big question for us, when we reach adulthood, or wake up, should not be "What am I going to do?"

A better question is "What sort of humangee am I going to be?"

Am I going to live as a people pleaser, fulfilling the opinions of others? Am I going to sell my essence for the material possessions of the world?

Or am I going to be true to myself, and do the best with what I have been given?

A Philosophy for My Life

We need to have a philosophy for our lives, as opposed to obtaining a series of roles, occupations, and events to fill them. We must each define how we wish to live and how we wish our lives to unfold. Otherwise, life will be a series of random events where we drift like a lost driver on small country roads, going here and there, unclear on our direction. Are we to be steered by matters and events outside our control?

Without having a north star, or a philosophical compass, we drift. We face the risk of an unfulfilled, lethargic life. Lying on our deathbed, we may wonder, *What if?*

Without a philosophy, without this decision, how do humangee make correct choices as to how to live?

We are all designed to add value and to have an impact, no matter how small we may perceive that to be.

||

A Case of Mistaken Identity

Questions haunt us:

Am I in the right career or is something else my life's work?

Why do I often feel so empty, no matter how much money I have or how successful I have become?

With our mistaken identity—our ego—we take ourselves and the events in our lives far too seriously. Life is full of have to's. We do many things, but we do not love to do them.

Burdened by the have to's, we yearn for something else.

Dread

We are afraid to live our lives truly and fully. We have sold out for a false security of material possessions and how others see us.

We become preoccupied with increasing our net worth, getting a newer, bigger car, but we gain nothing of real significance. These ideas lead us by the nose, and we are slaves to them.

We are dominated by fear and the result of fear is that our lives are much smaller than they are meant to be.

Fear grows
if you avoid and move away

What has changed that has converted the awe and wonder we felt as children into fear as adults?

Like in the school playground, we are frightened to leave the crowd. We want to fit in, not to stand out. We are afraid to listen to the call of our hearts and try new things.

Incongruence

We live our lives in a subconscious hurt, knowing that we are not being true to ourselves. To forget this discomfort, we distract ourselves with company and activity. We never want to be alone. We fill our lives to keep out the silence and stillness because, in that silence and stillness, we know we are living untrue to ourselves.

So, our lives are filled with new activities; we are constantly trying out new things. We plan our holidays, add on to our houses, buy new furniture, redecorate, make social plans, live for the weekend and the summer.

Every year brings new fads, and we participate. We don't want to be left behind. Some joke that shopping is cheaper than therapy.

We talk about other people and things when all that is needed is to take stock of ourselves, wake up, and take action.

The Need for Acceptance

This is exemplified with our newfound best friend, our mobile phones. We desire to be part of groups, and we need to see responses to everything we post.

We react like puppets to requests for likes, and we jump at every opportunity to be recognized and accepted by our online friends. This part of life has become a hankering for online validation and involvement with e-friends and followers. It is another vicious cycle into continuous attachment.

It's not really the device, it's the desired outcomes, the recognition and endorsement. The phone is simply a delivery medium for the desire-laden content.

We focus on what is missing in our lives rather than all that we are blessed with.

We Postpone Living Now

I will spend more time with my family when I get the promotion. I will, I promise. But we never do because we have learned to postpone. When the time comes, we just postpone again.

We have so many plans for the future. We are so sure we are going to get them. None of us plan to die even though it is inevitable.

Mediocrity

So, we live in mediocrity. We believe we are not meant for miracles. We play small. We become average fathers, average mothers, mediocre spouses, lethargic friends. We make so much of trivial things, make the unimportant important and the important unimportant. Most of the time we are simply not where our bodies are.

We are unavailable, caught up in our mental and emotional worlds. Life is calling us but we are not there to pick up.

Unexamined Lives

Our lives are full of unexamined assumptions (e.g., wealth is better than poverty, birth is better than death, youth is better than old age).

Unexamined, these false assumptions run our lives. Living according to these false assumptions, our lives in turn are false.

We believe in scarce resources—so we hoard and grab. We believe in bad luck and injustice.

> In the end, the one person that we have lost contact with, the one person whom we have no relationship with, is ourselves. The spark is missing.
>
> We don't know who we are or what we are meant to be doing with our lives.

So, how are we to become congruent and alive?

1. Practice Self-inquiry

Before there can be any change in our lives, we need awareness. Awareness of the present moment. Awareness makes choice possible, and with choice comes the possibility of change.

Self-examination is required if we are going to drop the false and be true to ourselves. Challenge yourself. What will you no longer tolerate in your behavior, thoughts, and feelings?

Do not accept any behavior, any thoughts, any feelings that limit you. Be awake to those that take away from your happiness and that deny the truth about yourself— overeating, unsupportive habits, thinking you are inferior.

> Elevate your life through self-inquiry and conscious action. If we do not do this inner work, all our fears and limiting ideas will rule our lives. It takes courage to explore oneself, but it is also the greatest, most exciting, and most rewarding endeavor we will ever undertake.

2. Serve Others

Make time every day to be of service to others. Help people to fulfill their dreams, as many have helped you to fulfill yours. Ask, how can I serve others better today?

We are here to enrich the world. We are here to serve the force that sent us into the world. When we serve others, the creation then takes care of us. Make other people's lives better. As you sow so shall you reap.

WC Stone said that you can have anything you want in life if you help enough other people get what they want.

3. Become Fearless

We are often afraid to leave the familiar and meet the unknown. The unknown is new and exciting; it is not to be feared. While there may be little or no known structure in the unknown, moving toward it without fear brings freedom.

Such is our insecurity that many of us prefer to be a prisoner rather than regain our freedom. Even if we taste freedom, we often return to our safe but discontent prison of the familiar.

When we are old, what fills us with regret are not the risks that we took but the opportunities we did not seize—all the things we did not do. The failure to try is the greatest fiasco of all.

Always forgive yourself your mistakes so that you can move on. We need to learn from our mistakes. We must face our fears because in facing them, we transcend them.

Question everything. Set aside that which does not stand to reason, that which deadens you, that which dims your light.

Fear shrinks as you tackle and move towards it

4. Cultivate Stillness

We see the world not as it is, but as we are. If only we can be still, we see things as they are. All it takes to start is pausing regularly and coming into the present. Once we begin to listen to life, then our lives will work better. We need to be still to listen.

We cannot discover our destiny by thinking about it. Our destiny will discover us, and we will only recognize it when we are still.

Rebuild your true relationship with yourself. Get to know the workings of your body, mind, and heart. Find out what you really value.

Let life lead you rather than you pushing it.

The biggest mistake is not to listen to yourself. Only in stillness can we hear our true selves.

5. Work with Nature, Not Against

The wise humangee works with nature—his/her own nature and the nature of the universe. We must understand the universal laws governing our world and align our lives to them. Then our lives work naturally and automatically.

Something then happens. Life becomes charmed. It is like we are being guided. The universe then supports us on our journey. The more we stop trying to force things to happen, the more the magic will return to our lives. We cannot force the good to happen; we can only allow it.

We must practice letting go of our own rushed pace. Discover nature's timing. It's not going to unfold as we wish but as nature allows. We are so arrogant. We think we are more intelligent than the universe. Working with natural laws makes life simple.

Fear, resulting in the desire to control, is one of the most influential factors in causing us to live untrue to ourselves. So, release control over your life. Ask yourself why you want to control your life. Why do we need to know how our lives will turn out?

Every one of us has something to contribute. We all came into this world to serve and to add value and we are fully equipped to fulfill this task. Our talents will naturally fulfill our purpose.

We have the responsibility to discover a suitable role and live it; this enriches our life and the lives of others.

Do everything excellently, particularly the small things. With this we gain self-respect.

Do not make the mistake of doing nothing until you find a calling or passion. Start to serve now in some small way and grow it from there.

Everything then satisfies. Satisfaction is not in what we do, but how we do it. We, then, begin to feel good about ourselves.

6. Idealism

In truth humangee is perfect. S/he is ideal. If we serve idealism, dormant forces, faculties, and talents come alive. We discover that we are far greater than we ever thought we were, and limiting thoughts are broken forever.

Idealism fills and engages our hearts. Think of how much in our lives our heart does not fully support. Once there is an emotional engagement around an activity, the passion in our lives returns and energy overflows. Each of us should have a compelling cause to live for.

Humangee can only express greatness if sparked by inspiring ideas, powered by love and understanding. Nobody with small ideas has ever attained greatness. When men and women have served great and universal ideas, they have become immortalized in the memories of mankind and they have inspired and uplifted the world.

Think of Mandela with his idealism of forgiveness, Gandhi with the idealism of non-violence, and Mother Teresa loving and caring for those in need. They successfully achieved their aims by not abandoning true idealism. It is for this that they will be remembered for centuries to come. So, become a servant leader; join the ranks of those who served a cause greater than themselves. These are the great leaders.

Remember nature's time; all will come to pass, for unto everything there is a time. Be patient.

We see in Mother Teresa, Mandela, and Gandhi that patience, universal idealism, and virtue were the bedrock of their fulfilled potential. It can be the same for us and those we serve.

Conclusion

When we look within, we find our true self. Finding our true self, we find peace, love, freedom, and understanding. On finding these, we can now be true to ourself.

As Innies (inward-looking humangee), we live well, and living well, we will die well. Satisfied in life, we will be satisfied to leave it when the end comes. Don't wait the end of the journey for satisfaction; live daily in satisfaction and contentment.

To love yourself is to live an excellent life.

Do Your Best and Let Life Do the Rest

Ultimately, we are only answerable to ourselves.

To be successful is to live life in your own way as an authentic person. It is not about making a big change or doing nothing until the one big change presents itself. It is about uplifting our lives every day in some small way.

Humangeeogram – Life's Game

The Humangeeogram is a fun way to measure the extent to which you're uplifting your life day by day. We know that life can be interesting and challenging. Although we must work to earn money—we must have a means for providing for our own needs and wants, after all—we may view our work as service. There are variations in what is allocated to each humangee, with different baggage and attributes.

Given all this, our opportunity in life can be treated a bit like a game. It's a game of small improvements.

We can use a tool called a spider or radar diagram on a spreadsheet program like Excel or Numbers to clarify how the game may be played. It produces an output that looks a bit like a spider's web. To simplify this for you, I've set it up so you can play this game for yourself at www.humangee.net. Below, I will explain how this works.

Each humangee starts in life with some mental assets and attributes that may be perceived as good or bad—our initial programming. We grow up with a range of environments, parents, religions, locations, availability of shelter, food, love, friendship, education, and exposure to many aspects of life. By the time we are eighteen, humangee have developed into young adults.

By this stage we have some form of subjectively measurable Natural Life Profile, or *Humangeeogram. This is simply a list of twelve aspects or attributes* where each

may be given a perceived score. I have used a scale of 1–6 in the table below. Simply insert the score for each attribute in the associated box, and when they are all filled, press the button and the Humangeeogram is generated.

So, we can use this initial set of scores to generate our starting Humangeeogram for year 0.

Attribute Year 0	score
Responsibility for self	3
Unity	2
Service	2
Love of all	2
Resolution & commitment	4
Modesty & humility	3
Detachment	3
Awareness	3
Devotion to a greater good	2
Challenges accepted	4
Compassion	5
Stillness & practice	3

Humangeeogram - Year 0

The goal is to finish better than you started

Progress in the game is progress in natural life. All that is required are tiny improvements in each area over time, and the profile expands.

To succeed or win in the game one simply needs to make consistent genuine efforts to push your boundaries in aligning with the natural law and guideline areas. That's it.

That's all there is to it. You take the profile you were allocated coming in at year 0, apply the laws and rules, and leave it better than you got it.

The following list of attributes are some that I have selected as useful. There may be others that apply equally well and resonate with you and your humangee. Small positive changes across a few areas make a huge difference.

Attribute Year 5	score
Responsibility for self	6
Unity	3
Service	5
Love of all	4
Resolution & commitment	4
Modesty & humility	4
Detachment	4
Awareness	4
Devotion to a greater good	3
Challenges accepted	5
Compassion	6
Stillness & practice	4

Humangeeogram - Year 5

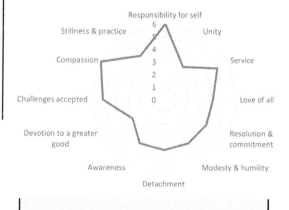

Chapter 18
Steps to Awareness

When humangee want or need to learn something, they go through a growth cycle. It starts at a low level of competence, cycles through a process of gaining knowledge, builds on that with insight and experience, and then engages in ongoing practice to achieve an acceptable level of competence.

Let's call this the **competence ladder**. Starting from unconsciously incompetent, they move through the process and stages to become unconsciously competent. They don't even have to think about it, as it has become ingrained and comes easily to them.

Let's use learning to drive a car as an example:

- John can't drive. He gets his trainee driver license, and then books some lessons. The driving instructor picks him up, they go to the car, and John proceeds to get in the wrong door. After he gets in the correct door, the instructor holds onto the key until John has learned what the controls are for because the instructor realizes that John doesn't know what he doesn't know. He is at the level of ***unconsciously incompetent***.

- The first day, he learns some basics about the pedals and the controls, and soon John is allowed to try driving in a controlled area. He goes slowly so that he won't damage the car or other drivers. As this progress continues, the instructor soon allows John to go out on the open

road. Around this stage, John moves on to ***conscious incompetence***. He is still incompetent, but now he is aware of how much he still has to learn.

- After further practice driving on open roads, John is now able to do most of the maneuvers required and is getting close to being ready to do his driving test. He is now at the stage of ***consciously competent***. He knows what to do, but it is still relatively new and has not yet formed a mental habit. He can be a little bit unsure in certain circumstances.

- John takes and passes the test, getting access to a car. He drives it daily, and much of this is city driving. After six months, it's like he has been driving for years. He is now ***unconsciously competent***. He can go through the motions of driving with very little thought, as most of the procedures and responses now come naturally to him. He is competent, and he doesn't even have to think about it. He has scaled the competence ladder with regard to learning to drive a car.

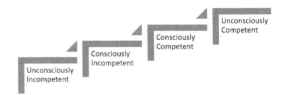

The process of humangee awakening is similar. We'll call this an **awareness ladder**.

Most human devices are aware that they are able to observe their body and also their mind, but they don't know how they really operate. The level of awareness or awakeness depends on the individual device and observer, with most starting **unconsciously unaware**.

Only when compared to being still and mindful do we start to appreciate that, to a large extent, our periods of being fully awake and aware are quite limited.

Let's explore this process in more detail.

Extended Awareness Ladder: Steps to a Good Life

Step 1: Humangee should aspire to wisdom: Why?

Philosophy – the love of wisdom

- Provides well-established knowledge
- Gives car directions on good actions
- Sets out the Why and the How

Step 2: Humangee starts to wake up

Recognize the present moment and the inner world

- The more we go deep, the more we are aware
- Impossible to grow in wisdom when bound by fear and anxiety
- Appreciate the present moment, pausing, attention to the task in hand, being mindful and a longer stillness and breathing practice (2–3 mins)

Step 3: Learns to be aware

Humangee comes to know self

- Make a habit of the practice – 10-20 second pause, fall still
- Notice how desires arise, your own or someone else's
- Contemplation and balanced reflection calms
- Increase in good thoughts
- Appreciate and express your gratitude
- Make a study of distinctions between mind, heart, body
- See how the attention operates: centered or open or not?
- Take regular time for pauses and dedication

Step 4: Aware of the unchanging

Recognize the stillness below

- Be there when the event takes place (de-stress by letting go)
- The way to meet the need of the moment
- There is no life other than the life that is being lived now
- Awake and enjoy
- Peace and clarity come when the attention is centered
- Decrease in bad thoughts
- Observe bodily movement and your senses
- Claim nothing; enjoy

Step 5: Aware of beauty – it shines in every single thing

Beauty is wonderous to encourage connection with the senses

- Look out for something beautifully done
- Observe how love and beauty are so closely linked
- Retrain mind to look with the eye of the artist or purist
- Appreciate great ideas, concepts, creations, people
- The recognition of beauty externally stimulates the appreciation within
- Without beauty in the observer, none can be found outside

Step 6: Serenity is more prevalent

Become alert to your state of awareness

- If humangee mind is dull and heavy, is the heart cold and closed?
- If agitation exists and your mind is restless, this does not serve those around you
- Be aware of these states that rule the heart, mind, and body
- Any unnecessary thoughts or agitation – remember, "Let it go"
- Use of reflection and peaceful state of mind
- Experiment with the guidelines (be awake and observe the effect)

Step 7: Love and self-care for humangee

Communion means coming together, as one

- Inner communion indicates a returning home to the center of one's being
- Care for your body, mind, and heart
- Confront the constraints that confine us
- Wisdom is dependent on the level of being & thus self-remembering (awakeness)

- Simple beauty is discovered in simple things
- Never dismiss yourself as unworthy

Step 8: Inner progress

Nowhere can humangee find a quieter, more untroubled retreat than in its own soul or essence

- Balance and measure in activities, approach, and consumption
- Notice the everchanging balance of the state of awareness in the being (in yourself)
- Be conscious of how the light of being awake illuminates
- Self-discipline is self-love
- Make small consistent efforts
- Use the practice(s) to remember your essence
- Decrease worldly attractions

Step 9: A fresh new dawn

No effort in this work is ever wasted

- Every day, every hour, every minute is new – Eternity's sunrise – not every day, but in every moment
- Meet people afresh and greet them as if for the first time
- Don't spend time in archives of past thoughts and anxieties
- The light of reason illuminates the present
- Give up those deep-rooted ideas you hold about yourself
- Ask yourself what you are serving in any situation
- Give up exclusively worldly objectives

Step 10: Love your humangee as someone you really care about!

Earnestly look after your humangee to the best of your ability and circumstances

- You'll reap satisfaction and freedom in the most important way
- You become an inner winner and learn the truth about yourself
- Happy in yourself, that happiness spreads
- Seeing self in all creatures and all creatures in self, you know no sorrow
- Seek out the uniting factor and act from that
- Freedom from thoughts about one's own self and one's personal profit

Message in Chipotle

A humangee had a wise teacher-coach at college who gave her some guidance as she was maturing and inquiring about life. Not long before the humangee graduated and moved away to work, they were sitting in a Chipotle restaurant discussing the challenges and opportunities of life. The coach took out a small neat clear plastic envelope with a folded color card inside, and said to humangee, "This is only to be opened in a time of extreme challenge and need. It may be a case or situation when it looks like there is no way out." Humangee was inquisitive about what it might say but did not ask. They discussed some concepts and events a bit further, finished their meal, and left.

Years later, humangee had worked hard and attentively to gain knowledge and skills and had built a business. But due to a series of events, she was now faced with bankruptcy; she was on the cusp of losing everything she had worked for over the years. Things looked bleak and impossible, and she was so low that she considered committing suicide. At this point she remembered the note her friend and coach had given her, and she got it out. She was in a state of despair and thought, I have kept it all these years, I may as well open it now. She carefully opened the envelope and unfolded the small card. Inside it read, "This too shall pass." After reading this, she became still and relaxed and her mind became clear.

Over the following weeks and months, she found a way to save the business, and it continued to grow from strength to strength. Her grateful, empowered employees decided to have a celebration party for her and her team. She had an executive board member mentor who was invited to attend also.

At the party, she was excited and happy, having helped turn the business and the fortune and future of her staff around. She thought, I am a winner. She was proud and happy. During the party, her mentor came up to her and suggested that she look at the note again, as they had discussed it before. She replied, "I am a heroine. People are celebrating our turnaround in the face of impossible obstacles. I'm not in despair or in an extreme or hopeless situation." But she took the advice, realizing that the message applies not only when things are bad, but also in times of victory and celebration.

She opened the envelope and the note and read, "This too shall pass." Again she fell still and her mind became clear.

It was as if a light had come on, and she recognized that nothing and no feeling is permanent. As day changes to night, so moments of despair and joy replace each other. She then learned to accept them both as a natural part of life. She understood that life experiences are often two-sided coins, comprising many opposing pairs or types of events: pleasure and pain, joy and sorrow, winning and losing, excitement and deflation, anger and compassion.

Hey, Coach, can you pass me the hot sauce?

Chapter 19
Life Gives Exams: Setting Expectations

Who sets our expectation for what life will be like and what we should expect?

It's a big responsibility, and our caregivers and teachers have room for improvement. However, even if they set our expectations perfectly, the humangee would need to be sufficiently awake to hear and take them on board.

The big elephant in the room is that of dysfunctional mental health across the humangee population. We try to explain this reality by applying fancy labels and diagnoses, but the reality is that a high proportion of humangee are not aligned with the natural system. As a population, we are not as mentally (or physically) healthy as we could be.

Most of the population are unclear on what to expect from life and how to handle it. An error by omission is that life will be anything other than a set of challenging and "interesting" events. Our current paradigm fails to make a clear distinction between the intrinsic aspects of our existence and the extrinsic aspects. Therefore, we fail to understand what is within our control and what is not.

Challenges are normal; they're to be expected. Humangee must accept this and address those challenges as they arise. Easier said than done.

Because of these false paradigms, life doesn't go as expected. There will be heartbreaks, disappointments, calamities at many stages on the journey. But if we realize they are simply a plot device within the play, then we can participate without being weighed down by them.

The journey of this life is by default an up-and-down adventure. It will not be perfect, it will have unknowns and surprises. There will be good and bad days and weeks. There will be challenges with relationships, with work, and with stresses and strains in most other aspects of our lives. But we are, or can be, perfectly equipped to navigate these.

We have a device that is a complimentary balance of inner and outer worlds, that is naturally designed to operate perfectly, if we allow it, or awaken it.

If we choose to continue operating under imbalance, we should understand the not-so-pleasant consequence.

If, on reading and absorbing this manual, you understand the game and the rules, then you have got to the stage of cracking part of the puzzle.

You now have the opportunity to get out of whatever hole you're in and start playing the game properly. Or you can go from one hole to a less deep one.

Just remember that this life is a journey, and it is easier to face it knowing that you are not alone, that you are on it with others. Purely by making internal progression, you are winning.

That is all that is required. Small advancements (even 0.01%), in multiple areas, accumulate over time. They are the difference between night and day.

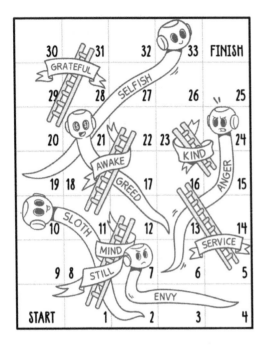

This is a version of a board game called Snakes and Ladders. Instructions on how to play the game are on the website www.humangee.net. The ladders' characteristics help you in achieving the goal and completing the task. The snakes are counterproductive, preventing you from getting to the finish, which is fulfillment.

Call to Action

The fantastic news is that if the wider populace, and particularly the younger generation, embrace this challenge, there is a life of adventure ahead and an opportunity to change the world. We have an opportunity to change mental health en masse across our planet. Together we can make this world into an even more wonderful place to enjoy the play.

We have at our disposal a wonderful set of resources. Our collective aim is to use them together for good.

An Eventful Journey

For many humangee, life is a struggle, and there are many factors that make it so. Escaping from that struggle can be challenging.

Getting access to the right environment, the right content, the right mentors and support, has historically not been easy or straightforward.

The good news is that if you can wake up to reality and learn to be present, then you are on your way. You simply follow the process and a transformation can take place over time, with consistent work. We then owe it to our brothers and sisters across the planet to help a few of them do likewise.

What Exams?

In a strange way, life is a form of education with continual assessment. The examination and assessment take into account that each humangee's starting point differs, and where and how you finish is relative.

As they say in sports psychology, the only win required is the win against the self. Your job is to uncover your best self.

For life, there are essentially three types of exams.

1. **Continuous assessment.** Daily opportunities to be awake and demonstrate what you have learned. To choose not to get agitated, and to recognize when you are self-selecting misery over happiness.

2. **Intermediate progress assessments.** Bigger challenges offering you the opportunity to reflect back over time and see where you have come from. When people study this material for a few years, the changes are generally noticeable and significant—to the positive.

3. **Big projects and key challenges or hurdles to get past.** These are some of life's big challenges that can often make or break a humangee. When you are equipped with the tools, you are ready, willing and able for any of these challenges.

Life, like any exam, should be challenging but fair.

And it is. (When one sees the big picture.)

Like the parable of the talents, more is expected from those who have been given more.

But like any teacher of a class, the main thing you want to see is some effort from your students. It is only with this effort that you as a teacher can facilitate their growth, support them, and help them blossom. It is easier for the creation and nature to provide help to those who actually seek it and want it.

Are you ready for the test?

■■

Unintentionally Misinformed?

Many parents and teachers try to guide their children to well-paying, safe careers because they appreciate that life can be challenging.

While they may understand the humangee hierarchy of needs (chapter 3), most live in a world where the focus is on external success rather than internal success.

There is no malice intended, it's just that many don't appreciate the difference and the true pros and cons for each route (external = transient, internal = permanent).

This is just the tip of the uninformed iceberg. Many other delusions and lies are offered in the form of well-intentioned advice from the paradigm of someone who only sees part of the picture.

All parents do their best, based on their view of the world. Each child growing to adulthood must take responsibility for reviewing their own position when they wake up.

Sample Reality Checks

So, in the theme of life exams and challenges, here are a few delusions that should be called out.

Delusion 1: I will make plans and they will work.

Anyone over a certain age knows that plans are not absolute—they are only guidelines, and we can be pretty sure that, depending on the size and duration of the project, the

■ ▶ ■

plans will change. Projects don't generally go exactly to plan. Our opportunity is to recognize this in advance and build in the ability to work around the twists and turns that will inevitably emerge. And sometimes a significant change of plan is required.

Delusion 2: I can have a life where my emotional heart will not be badly hurt.

For most people who live in the externally focused world, it is a fact that they will experience an emotional roller coaster, and some of the highs will be quite high, and some of the lows will be very low. An awake humangee does not suffer these swings and still enjoys a fulfilling emotional life.

Delusion 3: I can be immune to major challenges or difficulties.

Life is full of events, many that will seem gargantuan and life-changing. Some will be difficult and impose real trials of one's character. It's simply a fact of life that these will appear. To the unawake mind, they require soul-searching and often induce much anguish. We should not be surprised when they arrive. We can even take the opportunity to prepare properly. Most do not invest the time or effort. But we have a choice. We have the opportunity to see who or what (big me or little me) turns up to face them and in what manner (awake or asleep).

The Life and Death of a Fish

A humangee mother and her young child were sitting on the riverbank one day, homeschooling, during the COVID-19 era. Young humangee's granny had just died and they were both very sad. They were watching the river flowing gently by, with the ripples brushing gently against the branches and the grassy bank edge.

All of a sudden, a beautiful fish jumped out of the water and into the air. It was elegant and smooth, and it even looked like it was smiling. But no sooner was it up and out of the water, it disappeared back into the water again. The little humangee was dumbstruck. The fish was only with them for a second, and then it was gone again.

The young humangee said, "Mommy, the little fish is gone now. Is it dead too, just like Granny?"

The mother thought for a moment and said, "No, dear, the fish is just like Granny. Its appearance is just like life. Granny's soul still lives on. Just because you go back from whence you came does not mean that the true you is dead." And on they went with their day.

Born
What you come in with   LIVE A LIFE   Die
What you go out with

Conclusion

In section 1 we covered how the Earth and humangee evolved. And how we are all part of a natural universe determined by a set of natural laws and principles. This is consistent and proven across all major fields—physics, metaphysics, astronomy, natural science, biology, philosophy, and mathematics.

The natural laws and foundational philosophic and religious systems have been observed over many years and are collectively consistent over time. This is particularly true when we focus on the high level of similarities and commonalities across all. We overviewed the hierarchy of humangee needs starting from basics of food and security up to higher levels of self-awareness and being. We examined how the study of physics (physical sciences verifiable by our senses) and metaphysics (the reality beyond our physical senses) both point to a unified field, a unity that aligns with the universe. And when aspects are allowed to work as designed, harmony results.

We then looked at a functional model of the humangee operating system, to observe how the various aspects operate. This included assessing how our senses, components, and mind aspects function, as well as how they work together. These have been validated through observation over time.

When we looked at the core aspects of the mind, each appears to have a natural state, which is optimal when the device is operating correctly or naturally.

The operation of humangee as a single **body-mind-heart-nature-essence-observer** device is consistently demonstrated through daily experience, collective teachings, and observations over many years.

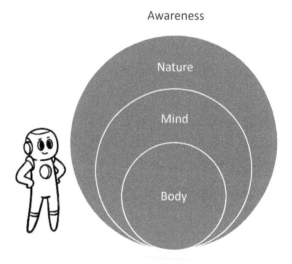

The net result is a set of recommendations for each component or function covered in section 2.

Many humangee spend a significant part of their waking lives thinking about the future or past. They are not present, in the now, for much of the time. This is fundamental to many of the problems that arise. They build worries, hopes, and fears in the future and harbor regrets, memories, and irritations from the past. Both good and bad thoughts take them out of the present, and they don't realize that there is a problem with this. We classify this existence in the past or future as an illusion or a dream state. Whereas being truly present, with attention focused on what is in front of us, is *present living*, where we are truly awake.

The very nature of the human life is "flea trained" at the start (chapter 7). By virtue of being a humangee, one is provided with a physical body-based device, in a world full of humangee and other physical things. The humangee primary sense organs are all oriented to the physical aspects of the being and its environment: sight, touch, smell, hearing, taste. A sense-being moving among sense-objects.

In essence, all humangee are the same and want the same: contentment, fulfillment, love, freedom, and truth.

We have the opportunity to see life as one of competition or as a wide form of collaboration.

How you live it and how you see it is important.

An Actor in a Play, a Player in a Game

It is helpful to make a distinction between the life (inner-life) and the life situation (outer-life).

The humangee by nature has an inner essence that is pure, perfect, and complete. The *humangee life* evolves one way, toward fulfillment, if the rules are uncovered or known and lived by. If they are unknown, ignored and not lived by, discontentment and suffering ultimately ensues for that humangee.

Life on the planet is a playground, where the humangee can interact and evolve individually and collectively, and their device or devices either purify or putrefy to the extent that they align with the natural laws.

When the true nature of this internal (subtle/mental) life is seen, experienced, and lived, it is a thing of simplicity, order, consistency, and perfection.

Ours is a perfectly designed game, with a fantastic array of creatures and characters, in a wonderful evolving, magical environment. As a play, it stretches in every direction from horror show to comedy, from romantic comedy to tragedy—billions of interlinked humangee, lives, adventures, discoveries, and life sub-plots that would make any soap opera producer proud. And it's full of the widest array of characters one could imagine, from villains and baddies to heroes and dreamers.

In reality, the life situation for most is hard. We have nearly eight billion humangee on a planet, essentially all wanting the same thing. Why wouldn't there be competition, and all the challenges that that brings as a consequence? We may take it as a given that life as a humangee can be challenging, with varying opportunities for pleasure and pain, happiness and misery, and that all are at different stages of a similar journey.

However, if we know and live the rules, we can evolve to our full humangee potential, increasing in joy, satisfaction, contentment, every day of every month of every year. If we can do this collectively, everything can be changed.

The humangee has the truth-seeking characteristics of an Exocet missile. The pain and challenges of the hardship in the life-game enable it to soul-search and see inward, beyond its physical body. When it has sufficiently uncovered the truth of the game and understands the "Why," it has the opportunity to complete the task.

It is not always easy.

But that does not mean you can't enjoy the journey.

Personal Awakening Precedes Mass Awakening

The good news is that, when operating naturally, humangee function consistently well with all the other aspects of the universe, at both a hardware and software level.

The bad news is that, for the most part, our conditioning and inability to live in the present means that we are not aligned to live in harmony with the physical world.

- Our discursive mind runs rampant and uncontrolled
- True reason is only able to operate occasionally
- Ego is largely unmanaged
- Heart holds unnecessary attachments and emotions
- We become puppets of reaction, unable to respond
- We misunderstand love and limit it only to a few

- The collective effects of this give us the dysfunctional external world that we live in today

Some humangee will be awake to understand these elements and the refinements that need to be implemented. Most will not.

The one thing we can do and have control over is ourselves. If we work on ourselves, then bigger change can and will happen.

Nature will then help us.

A Word about Practical Philosophy

This book was inspired by students and tutors of the School of Practical Philosophy and Economic Science in Ireland. There are too many to mention. Several have had a profound impact on this humangee journey.

This manual includes some insights and a distillation of observations from the numerous lectures made available for free by the school, for the good of all, including those from Mr. Shane Mulhall.

As mentioned in the manual, there are various places where one can go for direction in life. In this humangee's opinion, one of the best options is through the study of practical philosophy. It is the love of wisdom and the search for truth. It helps uncover the path to a more contented, balanced, loving, harmonious, and fulfilled life on Earth.

More details are available at:

- www.practicalphilosophy.ie
- www.practicalphilosophyonline.org
- www.humangee.net

Disclaimer

You now know the rules. You are responsible for your humangee. Any likeness to anything or anyone portrayed in this book is purely coincidental. ☺

This is not medical advice. It's an attempt at provoking self-responsibility, self-awareness, and life advice—for your consideration. There will no doubt be some who believe that they or their humangee do not fit this mold. And it is understood that their programming will accommodate that.

Life is a play and a game played in our minds and hearts. We can wallow and bicker that we can't play or don't want to play because we don't know the rules. Or that we are no good because someone inherited a better humangee than us. If you are reading this, you are in the game. We are no longer in the school playground. The real opportunity and fun in the game is as an adult. The real measure and currency of the game is not external, it is internal.

It is vital that you appreciate that we all inherit a humangee with different baggage and pre-existing programming. The bodies, environments, appearances, physical and intellectual traits, parents, friends, and other factors all vary hugely. But that's the fantastic element of the game.

It's not what you start with, it's what you do with what you've got.

Our opportunity in life is to see what we can do with what we have been allocated. The real happiness and contentment lie in the journey, knowing that you are living by the laws, doing the best that you can. For many it is a huge step. Many won't wake up sufficiently, or make the effort to bridge the gap.

Humangee custodian-observers now have the opportunity to appreciate that you don't truly live in your house, drive in your car, wear your trendy clothing; *you live in, drive, wear, are one with your humangee.*

Hence it is worth stepping back to understand the derivation of happiness, love, fulfillment and freedom.

Know in truth that you are already pure, perfect, and complete.

It's not what your humangee has; it is who or what your humangee becomes, or more correctly, is able to uncover in the process. To observe and experience the inner essence.

If, as humangee observers, we do our job well, we will be content in knowing that we did the best job that we could. We will lead a content life. We will leave with less baggage than we came in with.

Appendix 1
Validate, Understand, and Take Action

The following summary provides a list of some of the key recommendations that emerged throughout the manual. These can be complemented by those in the Not-So-Quick Start Guide in Appendix 2.

1. Appreciate that you can manage your device, but it does take consistent effort.
2. Investigate further to really understand and live by the eternal laws and principles.
3. Understand the distinction between "noise" and "stillness."
4. Appreciate that you are more than your body, mind, and heart. You are the observer as well.
5. Body, mind, heart, nature, essence, observer is a single functional unit.
6. Turn to self-inquiry to get a better understanding of who and what you are, and what you are here for.
7. Understand the aspects of service, responsibility, and love.
8. Recognize aspects of heart, ego, desire, and true reason, as well as discursive mind.
9. Observe your energy states and appreciate the impact that they have on your daily life.
10. Appreciate that there are more fundamental similarities between the world's religions, races, nationalities than differences.
11. Understand and utilize the concept of the play and the practice of detachment.
12. Practice noticing. Attention is a critical aspect of how we live and operate. Understand how it works.
13. Realize that when we are awake and present, happiness, misery, compassion, and love are conscious choices.
14. Be present. Daily practice is required to embed the various mechanisms to come into the present.
15. Work through the refinement process on an iterative basis (repeating and refining).
16. Recognize the difference between the mind-focused external world (transient) and a stillness-focused internal world (permanent-eternal).
17. Accept life—all of it. There is no point in resisting it. Resisting results in friction.
18. Review your values and paradigms.
19. Practice care in language and speech, both self-talk and with others.
20. Look after both your body and mind as best you can.
21. Be awake to error signals. Take action to address them.
22. Understand that you get what you focus on.
23. Realize that it's not okay to be a thinking addict. It undermines your ability to be present and thus live your true life.
24. Appreciate the concept of the present moment and awake living in the present. Live your life now.
25. Find the permanent happiness inside rather than the temporary one outside.

26. Understand there are few things in life over which humangee has control. Emotions are one of them.

27. Learn to observe when your mind is attached to something: a thing, an irritation, an event. Learn to let go as appropriate.

28. Live with love in the heart and reason in the mind if you wish to be a happy humangee.

29. Realize that we are here to serve. True service is dedicated to something greater than oneself.

30. Take responsibility for yourself and others.

31. Respond rather than react.

32. Remember that love, gratitude, and kindness are contagious.

33. Observe and manage ego and desires.

34. Understand that happiness arises in desirelessness.

35. Practice awareness exercises: pause, sense checks, mindfulness, meditation, and others.

36. Question your false beliefs and inappropriate paradigms.

37. Trust that if you follow the process, the journey can be fun, irrespective of the situations encountered.

38. Do your best and let life do the rest.

39. Connect with your essence. You are pure, perfect, and complete.

40. Love yourself; to love yourself is to live an excellent life.

41. Detach. See and enjoy your life as a play; you and all around you will benefit.

42. Make a distinction between your life and your life situation.

Appendix 2
Humangee and Epictetus

Quick Start Guide

A summary of his recommendations is used as the basis of this Not-So-Quick Start Guide.

Epictetus, one of the world's early philosophers, lived at the turn of the first and second centuries. He was born as a slave. His master held a position in Emperor Nero's court and thus Epictetus gained firsthand experience of the manners, routines, and attitudes of the emperor and his courtiers. Later, Epictetus was granted his freedom, and he devoted himself to a life of philosophy.

The influence of Epictetus has been enormous. His philosophy influenced emperor and philosopher Marcus Aurelius, the development of Islam, Descartes, and current schools of thought including Cognitive Behavioral Therapy and Positive Psychology.

The chief concerns of Epictetus were integrity, self-management, and personal, inner freedom. He said that our convictions, attitudes, and intentions are truly ours in

a way that nothing else is. We may not be able to control what he called externals—for example what others do or say, or whether we may have good or bad fortune in the world—but we do have a choice as to how we respond to such matters. Our responses are internal, not external, and therefore are within our control.

> *"While there is only one thing we can care about and attach ourselves to,* we choose instead to care about and attach ourselves to a score of others: to our bodies, to our property... And, being attached to many things, we are weighed down and dragged along with them. What should we do then? Make the best use of what is in our power, and treat the rest in accordance with nature."* Discourses 1:1:14

When faced with a terrible fate (in his case imprisonment and execution) Epictetus said:

"What should we have ready at hand in a situation like this? The knowledge of what is mine and what is not mine, what I can and cannot do. I must die. But must I die bawling? I must be put in chains—but moaning and groaning too? I must be exiled; but is there anything to keep me from going with a smile, calm and self-composed?" **Discourses 1:1:21**

Where is progress, then? "If there is anyone who renounces externals and attends instead to their character, cultivating and perfecting it so that it agrees with *nature, making it honest and trustworthy, elevated, free, unchecked and undeterred;*

And if they've learned that whoever desires or avoids things outside their control cannot be free or faithful, but has to shift and fluctuate right along with them, subject to anyone with the power to furnish or deprive them of these externals;

And if from the moment they get up in the morning they adhere to their ideals, eating and bathing like a person of integrity, putting their principles into practice in every situation they face, that is where you will see true progress embodied..."
Discourses 1:4:18

What is our experience in relation to these choices? Are our choices really ours, or are they made for us by other people and the world? Do we really use our true faculty of reason?

We are told we have that choice. What is our experience?

This is an important question. For example, it is not uncommon that people think of themselves as victims, unable to exercise choice. It should not be denied that terrible things may happen to people and that these have their effects, which should be acknowledged with sensitivity.

However, is it possible to make other choices in how we see and respond to events?

A summary of his teachings, entitled *Enchiridion: A Manual for Living*, has been read and used across centuries by world leaders, generals, and ordinary people as a guide to serenity and moral direction amid the extreme trials of life.

Epictetus tried to answer two questions:
- How do I live a happy, fulfilling life?
- How can I be a good person?

Main themes:
- Mastering your desires
- Performing your duties
- Learning to think clearly about yourself and your relations with the larger community of humanity
- Allowing yourself to fall still, and connecting with the stillness that exists
- Appreciating your subtle being: you are more than just your body and mind and heart
- Living a happy life and a virtuous life are one and the same

The original translators, various authors, and scholars have interpreted, summarized, and contemporized the teaching of Epictetus in much more depth and clarity than done here. Hence, I would urge you to explore these in more detail, they include works by Chakrapani, Lebell, Harris, and others. The timeless principles of *The Enchiridion* clearly align with the themes and interlocking laws in chapter 4, as well as the mental model we've discussed. The following recommendations overlap and complement each other.

Purpose, Vision, Virtue, and Service
- Be true to yourself.
- Practice clear thinking so that you may be properly able to direct your will and be devoted to your true purpose.
- Cultivate awareness so that you may discover the connections you have to

others and clarify the duties that follow from those relationships.

- Build your own self-worth; it cannot be derived from an external source.
- Do not depend on the admiration of others.
- Do your own useful work, gathering ideas and opportunities from resources such as books, specialized knowledge, podcasts, tools, etc.
- Remember that character is independent of physical, intellectual, or other possessions.
- Grow up, be awake, and realize that it's not relevant what other people think about you.
- Focus your attention; be wary of myriad distractions.
- Plainly describe the person you want to be. Precisely articulate the demeanor you want to adopt. This facilitates you to live it, when by yourself or with others.
- Enable your personal vision and ideals by studying and appreciating suitable role models. We hold all the seeds of greatness within us.
- Consider the simple concept of virtue: ordinary, steady, day-to-day service for the good of all and thus self.

Responsibility

- Choose to respond rather than react: you may not always see it, but you always have a choice in how you respond to an event or action.
- Remember that clear thinking is vital.
- Know that a life of wisdom is a life of reason. It requires proper training and practice.
- Understand that interpersonal relationships reveal our duties to one another.

- Act on the truth that you are not an isolated entity but a unique and interconnected human being.
- Understand your relationships; remember to whom you are obligated within family, neighborhood, state, and humankind.

Natural Laws

- Understand the natural laws and the consequences of both living and not living them.
- Uncover moral progress and growth in truth.
- Seek freedom from inner turmoil as the path to true self-awareness.
- Trust that serenity is a clear sign of a good or higher life.
- Focus on keeping your will and actions in harmony with the truth, and be wary of the distraction of things that are not relevant to you.
- Adapt your wants and expectations to reality, including expectations that depend on others.
- Understand nature and natural laws as the path to aligning your intentions and actions with the way things are.
- Be the person who truly understands, applies, and takes action in line with these principles.
- See that life is our play: always act well the part which you have been allocated.
- Remember that you have the opportunity to give an impeccable performance, in whatever role you're given and for however long or short a time.

Unity, Essence, Spirit, and Alignment

- Understand that you are not what you have or "own."

171

- Steward and care for what you happen to have, but realize that you don't really have anything to lose.
- Accept the subtlety that when something is lost or stolen, "It has been returned to where it came from."
- Remember that awakening can be found through the seemingly big challenges.
- Understand that how you look at death, infirmity, loss, and disappointment are important.
- Remember that you can choose to see clearly; to free yourself of illusions and false hopes; and to avoid miserable, envious, or other unnecessary thoughts.
- Instill in yourself your vision of wisdom and goodness. Attach yourself to unity and what is naturally superior.
- Recognize that true awareness lies first in holding correct opinions and attitudes toward the planet and the universe.
- Know that unity is the antidote to bitterness and confusion.
- Trust that you are ready for anything you may face.
- View the world as an integrated whole, faithfully incline your whole being toward the highest good, and adopt the will of nature as your own.
- The universe's design is intelligent, natural, and fundamentally good.

Modesty, Humility, and Dignity

- Embrace modesty in all areas (e.g., avoid over-conspicuous displays of virtue, generosity, or goodness).
- Observe balance and good measure in food, clothing, housing, cars, relaxation, work, consumption, sleep, pleasure, pain, exercise, rest, etc.
- Reflect on the truth that decency and inner harmony are more valuable than appearance.
- Know that character is foundational and is more important than reputation.
- Delight in others who are doing well.
- Approach life as if it were a formal gathering. Be on time, polite, courteous, reserved, and unhurried.
- Know that if you wish to test yourself, do it for yourself—modestly, quietly, and without the need to impress others.

Acceptance versus Control

- Know what you can control and what you can't.
- Harmonize your actions with the way that life really is … in accordance with nature.
- Don't take things personally. Things don't just happen *to you*—they just happen.
- Understand nature and the natural laws and thus learn to appreciate and accept life's events, even death, with awareness and intelligence.

Clarity, Observation, and Presence

- Be awake to the preference of immediate gratification over enduring satisfaction. Consider that deliberation strengthens your character.
- Learn how to identify erroneous/misinterpreted thinking.
- Study how inferences are legitimately derived so that you avoid drawing unfounded conclusions.

- Be awake to your interpretation of events. Really open your eyes and other senses.
- Use "The Exercise" (take 1–10 seconds to pause and fall still).
- Discriminate between events and your interpretation of them.
- Remember that what hurts a person is not the event but the response that they have adopted.
- Avoid melodramatic reactions when you offer kindness and a sympathetic ear.
- Take respectful and diligent care of your body, but don't flaunt it.
- Avoid casual sex. Ideally, avoid sex before marriage. This demonstrates respect for self and others.
- Refrain from self-righteously promoting your own views.
- Hold back from automatically defending your reputation or intentions. Don't be afraid of verbal abuse or criticism.
- Carry yourself with dignity.

True Reason and Decision-Making

- Take a position once you have deliberated and applied true reason, but be open to being challenged and refuted.
- Appreciate and refine your ability to reason. Understand how to use this uppermost faculty of your mind.
- Realize that your body is secondary and subservient to your mind.
- Treasure your mind, and value clarity and awareness.
- Embrace events as they occur.
- Make full use of the events that come your way, which are often concealed as challenges.

- Trust that the challenges you undergo will teach and strengthen you.

Desires and Wants

- Be awake and clinically objective about understanding your desires.
- Understand that "wants" (as opposed to needs) place demands on you and rule your mind. And when you build "I don't want" aversions, they become an unintentional focus.
- Recognize that if you don't get what you want, you'll be disappointed; and if you get what you don't want, you'll be distressed.

Communication

- Exercise precision in how you describe or label things, events, or people. By using correct naming and assessment, you comprehend them correctly.
- Listen and talk with precision, but not dismissively, superciliously, or arrogantly.
- Recognize that wisdom is revealed through actions and deeds, not talk.
- Avoid discussing your higher or spiritual aspirations with people who will not appreciate them.
- Strive to be modest and noble.
- Endeavor to communicate with good purpose.
- Remember that the clear mark of moral power is right speech and that this takes work and effort.
- Pause and be present before you speak.
- Avoid glib talk; it disrespects others, like an uncontrolled vehicle heading for a ditch.

- Be cautious of the spirit and intent of your discussion; content should be worthy.
- Don't engage in common blathering that passes for worthwhile discussion; it has a corrosive effect.
- Realize that you become what you give attention to.
- Recognize that much of our TV and radio is dumbed down to become corrosive chewing gum for the mind.
- Be wary and awake to most popular entertainment, as some masquerades exploiting a whole range of human weaknesses.
- Notice how easy it is to unintentionally slip into inappropriate and vulgar engagement.
- Be awake to the company you keep; it's human and instinctual to imitate the habits of those with whom you interact.
- Consider how your small words and deeds are affecting your circle of influence.
- Ask whether you are doing your part to bring out the best in others.
- Understand the importance of discretion and observe it in conversing.

Happiness and Freedom

- Do not give your mind over to anyone.
- Notice how you unknowingly give your happiness away for free and decide instead to use it for your benefit, not your detriment.
- Accept life's limits and inevitabilities, and work with them; in this way you become free.
- Do not succumb to passing desires or freedom is lost.

- Know that your will is always within your control.
- Understand that other people's negative views are contagious and to be avoided.
- Remember that happiness can only be found within.
- Practice indifference to external conditions; aspire only to be your best self.
- Notice that your happiness depends on three things, all within your control: your will, your ideas, and what you make of your ideas.
- Know that authentic freedom places demands on us.

Substance, Form, and Delusion

- Observe appearances for what they are; understand that things are not as they appear to be.
- Remember that self-honesty is the foundation for self-mastery.
- Know first who you are and what you are.
- Trust that you are always learning and growing.
- Know that no one can hurt the essence of you. It is always your choice to view what is happening as insulting or not.
- Choose to respond rather than react; it is only your judgment of the incident that provokes you.
- Acknowledge and act on kind and generous impulses.
- Express your gratitude; withhold it is like wrapping a present and not giving it. Give the present. Say thank you when appropriate.
- Enjoy the attitude of gratitude, and realize that the opposite applies: a complainer is a drainer.

Misery

- Recognize that misery comes from mistakes in the form of false impressions. Understand that someone who mistreats you or makes this type of mistake does so based on that false impression.
- Don't fault, guilt, blame, undermine, or reprimand others (context is relevant).
- Remember that it's not events, deeds, or activities that torment us but our feelings about them.
- Understand that the impulse to blame or admonish others is foolish.
- Nurture the gradual extinction of blame.

Love Self and Love All

- Emphasize moral progress over moral perfection.
- Achieve moral progress by working on yourself daily.
- Inspire to make the small successive changes that culminate in personal dignity and a noble life.
- Bring your actions and desires into harmony with nature; this enables enduring serenity and freedom.
- Remember that it's not so much WHAT you are doing but HOW you are doing it.
- Look before you leap; walk before you run.
- Survey and test a prospective action before progressing.
- Stand back and take an objective look at the big picture.
- Think through potential hurdles and challenges before making an important decision or commitment.
- Recognize that a tentative or half-hearted spirit has no power.
- Focus on your own activities, business, or concerns; this enables freedom and clarity.

- Start living your ideals; live by these rules as if they were laws.
- Offer gentleness and compassion to those who make mistakes.
- Apply the fundamental natural rules to the events and opportunities presented in daily life.
- Accept that it is impossible to be free from error.
- Remember that you choose your attitudes and responses to events and circumstances.

Wisdom

- Do not try to seem too wise to others.
- Recognize that trying to please others is a hazardous trap.
- Understand that self-awareness is the mark that life and the creation expect us to aim for.
- Consider whether evil is a by-product of laziness or forgetfulness.
- Remember that wisdom depends on consistent and clear observance.
- Observe how help and harm (good and bad) come from within yourself.
- Disregard things beyond your control.
- Consider that true internal freedom is an innate aspiration in life.
- Remember that living wisdom is more important than knowing about it.
- Trust that everything happens for a good reason. All events contain advantage for you, if you just look for it.
- Understand that those who are different and follow the path of wisdom will be mocked and teased; expect it and carry yourself humbly and consistently.
- Don't consent to being hurt; this is a choice over which you have control.

Appendix 3
Humangee Software End Users License Agreement[8]

Your humangee contains factory-installed software programs.

Please read the Software License Agreement before proceeding to operate this equipment.

Rights in the software are offered only on the condition that the user agrees to all terms and conditions of the License Agreement. Proceeding to operate the equipment indicates your acceptance of these terms and conditions. If you do not agree with the terms of the License Agreement, you must now remove the Humangee Awakeness Module (HAM)—or it may be removed remotely.

There is no option to return the complete device for a full refund. Proceeding with configuration signifies your acceptance of the License Terms.

Unless otherwise stated below, this Software Product License Agreement shall govern the use of all software that is provided to you, the user, as part of the humangee product.

It supersedes any non-humangee software license terms that may be found online or in any documentation or other materials contained in the product packaging.

Note: Operating System Software by BIOCHA Bunnito is licensed to you under HMG End Users License Agreement (EULA).

The following License Terms govern the use of the software:

Use. User may use the software on any one device. User may not network the software or otherwise use it on more than one device. Customer may not reverse assemble or decompile the software unless authorized by law.

Copies and Adaptations. Customer may not make copies or adaptations of the software for archival or cryogenic purposes.

Ownership. User agrees that he/she does **not have any title or ownership** of the software or essence.

While the term *custodian* or *observer* is used in the document, the user can own the body (in as much as one can own anything) as it is simply a sophisticated vehicle-shell. However, they are simply a temporary custodian and observer of the essence.

Devices are simply held under license for the duration of their existence as live entities on Earth.

---

8 Satire intended.

* *

Caveats

Improper and prolonged use of input devices and storage components are among those tasks that have been associated with Misery Syndrome. If you experience continuous discontentment, you may want to look at if proper operation processes are being followed. (You may also want to check the disclaimer at the end of the manual.)

Appendix 4

Two Ends of the Continuum: Aligning with Natural Laws

Alignment	Mis-Alignment
Sees the bigger picture	**Sees only the limited picture**
Aware of both external and Internal aspects	Solely focused on External aspects
Focus on needs	Focus on wants
Dettached from the ego	Attached to the ego
I am not just my body-mind, it is an instrument for my use	I am my body, mind, ego, and identity
Being	Becoming
Live happy and content	I want to become happy - will be happy next year
I am enough	I want more
Attention focused on the task in hand - present	Attention often scattered and not focused or present
See unity and sameness everywhere	See duality and difference everywhere
Know and live eternal laws	Unclear on the eternal laws and rules
Exists in stillness	Exists in noise constant thinking and need for activity
Sufficiently present and clear on misconceptions and mistakes (Ch 10)	Not clear on misconceptions and mis-takes
Can observe and manage emotions	Unable to observe and manage emotions
Calm, focused, awake activity	Frenetic activity or lethargy
Make time to play - life is fun	No time to play - life is not a lot of fun
Aware of energy states - see mind model appendix	Unaware of energy states - 3 Guna
Has open mind and challenges paradigms	Tends to have a closed mind, fixed and rigid paradigms
Sees justice in operation everywhere	Sees injustice everywhere
Wise	Ignorance of insight
Selfless	Selfish

At a broader company, organizational, group, or country level	
Broader Natural | *Alignment*	**Broader | *Mis-Alignment***
Aware of nature and fundamentals	Oblivious, uninterested in natural law fundamentals
Has a natural moral compass and code	Overrides their natural moral compass and code
Aligned and balanced to natural aspects and cycles	Misaligned, unbalanced to natural aspects and cycles
Activities done with measure	Activities neglected or to excess
Respect for natural resources, cycles, and systems	No respect for natural resources, cycles, and systems
Operate for the good of all	Operate for the good of self
Take responsibility as custodian for the planet	Looter of the planet - take what I can get now
Minimise waste products - reuse versus replace	Dump old stuff, replace it with new stuff
Respect our biosphere and environment	Disrespect, pollute, dump - its less hassle for me
Protect our ecosystems	What relevance are ecosystems to me?

Appendix 5
The Happiness Billionaire

There was once a humangee happiness billionaire. She had many friends and was a modest, wise, engaging, and wonderful lady.

She was grateful for the hardships and inequalities she'd faced and the abilities and disabilities with which she had been bestowed. She knew that they had been instrumental in helping her on her journey to accumulate her wealth. She was getting old and had so much surplus happiness that she could never use it all. She had tried numerous times to give it away, but it just kept coming back and increasing. She decided to make a concerted effort to invest as much as she could in those who truly deserved it. She was not unduly concerned about those who wanted it, or those who felt they were due it, as they were many and often did not warrant it or had not earned it.

She would disappear for weeks on end and would transform into different personas. Initially, she was a sick younger person, then a sick older person, then she had various roles with little money. For a time, she took on the role of a victim of physical and mental abuse, a lonely teenager, then an isolated older person, then various unequally treated or disadvantaged members of society. She took lowly paid jobs with little or no security, often not particularly pleasant and sometimes with harsh conditions. She tried hospitality and health sectors as well as retail and backroom businesses to experience the ups and downs of each role and the surrounding people. It was hard, emotionally draining, and painful; but it was also truly inspiring.

It gave her insight into how various people behaved, how they treated each other (good and bad) and looked after each other. She saw the true heart of all those that she met on the way. She gained insights about who would use the resource well and who might not. She performed this due diligence in order to allocate the happiness capital appropriately.

When the time came to pass on her multi-millions, she knew exactly who she wanted to share them with. She retraced her steps and sought out those who treated her as an equal and showed her respect and dignity. She remembered those who stretched themselves to give more than they were comfortable with—whether of their time, their empathy, their money, or other means. She enthusiastically allocated to those who went that little bit further to help and to serve without the desire for recognition or reward, to those who were kind, loving, and generous with what they had. She invested in those that had big hearts. She especially loved those who were attentive and grateful for what they had, rather than those who focused on what they didn't have.

She passionately supported those with the biggest challenges who kept their focus on doing something small and uplifting each day, staying positive in the face of adversity. She knew that this approach would help them get over the ramp, where they would see, know, and appreciate that their contentment was their true wealth, freedom, and success. Over time, they could then invest in others.

She and her team have now successfully funded thousands of happiness beacons and contentment entrepreneurs. Some are on their second and third round of funding and are doing fantastic work. She is still seeking more suitable recipients, as the fund has recently been expanded.

She became known as the venture capitalist (VC) of happiness. She saw it as her role to provide the seed happiness investment for the next generation of contentment entrepreneurs and to nurture those displaying the spark of making a difference. Like a true VC, she invested in people and teams, not purely in ideas.

Acknowledgments

There are many humangee that have unknowingly contributed to this book—some by virtue of traveling part of the same journey alongside me. You have my sincerest thanks.

I would like to focus on a few who have provided specific inspiration, support, and focus in enabling this output.

To my mum (mom), you are my role model.

To Grosher at Keepdoodling, for bringing my pencil-scrawled incoherent amoebae to life. To my editor, Paige Duke, a Socratic dialectic sleuth, for your diligence in getting to the truth of what I was trying to convey and asking subtle but vital questions that continued to refine and make my efforts readable.

To Rob, Kristie, Erica, Tyler, and the team at Archangel Ink for your insight, patience, guidance, pragmatism, and care (and for putting my singing career on hold).

To the school and the dedicated student-tutors who give their time for free, for supporting journeys of self-inquiry. I have done my best to stay true to the principles. If there are any inconsistencies or misinterpretations, this humangee takes full responsibility for them.

To my wife and sounding board, Geraldine, who, in addition to making this possible, keeps me truly grounded in the external world and supports my ventures to, in her words, the "happy-clappy" internal world. You are my best friend, my navigator, and the humangee that has shown me the essence in all.

To our humangee children, Lee, Emma, and Ryan. Thank you for ensuring that this man appreciates the hierarchy of needs and the order of the home, in which I happily sit at the bottom of the pecking order. You have all played a special part in facilitating the observations of a practical philosopher as a householder, a husband, and a father, working and living in the real world.

Any householder's life, as opposed to a monastic or ascetic philosopher's life, has different complications and challenges. These challenges are our strict teachers.

Collectively, your contribution has helped reduce the covering on this humangee essence, letting that internal light shine brighter than ever before.

With gratitude and love,

Frank

Lightning Source UK Ltd.
Milton Keynes UK
UKHW031250120321
380233UK00007B/1521